S0-BNJ-001

PANORAMIC CHINA

PANORAMIC CHINA

PANORAMIC CHINA

Beijing
—The City and the People

FOREIGN LANGUAGES PRESS

First Edition 2005
Third Printing 2009

ISBN 978-7-119-04038-7

Published by Foreign Languages Press
24 Baiwanzhuang Road, Beijing 100037, China
Website: http: //www.flp.com.cn
Email Addresses: Info@flp.com.cn
Sales@flp.com.cn
Distributed by China International Book Trading Corporation
35 Chegongzhuang Xilu, Beijing 100044, China
P. O. Box 399, Beijing, China

Printed in the People's Republic of China

Introduction

China has 23 provinces, four municipalities directly under the Central Government, five autonomous regions and two special administrative regions. Due to geographical and topographical differences and climatic variations, each area has its own unique natural scenery. The mountains in the north of the country are rugged and magnificent, the waters in the south are clear and turbulent, the Gobi in the northwest shines brilliantly in the sunlight, the hills in the southeast are often shrouded in floating fog, green waves of sorghum and soybean crops undulate over the vast fields of the northeast, and the mountains in the southwest, with sequestered villages and terraced fields, look tranquil and picturesque.

There are 56 ethnic groups in China. The Han, making up the overwhelming majority of the population, mainly live in the eastern and central parts of the country, while many ethnic groups with smaller populations live in the west. In China, all ethnic groups, regardless of size, are equal and respect each other. Each ethnic group has its own folk customs, religious beliefs and cultural traditions, and most use their own language and script. Regional autonomy is practiced in areas where ethnic minorities live in compact communities. All the ethnic groups call themselves "Chinese." They are courteous and friendly. In the ethnic-minority areas, the quiet environment, quaint buildings, exquisite fashions, unsophisticated folk customs and hospitality of the local people hold a great appeal to visitors from afar.

China boasts 5,000 years of recorded civilization and a brilliant culture. The country is home to such world-renowned cultural treasures as the Great Wall, terracotta warriors and horses of the First Emperor of the Qin Dynasty, Mogao Grottoes at Dunhuang, and Ming and Qing imperial palaces and mausoleums, and large numbers of ancient architectural masterpieces, including temples, Buddhist pagodas, residential buildings, gardens, bridges, city walls and irrigation

works. There are also cultural relics unearthed from ancientsites, including painted pottery, jade ware, bronze ware, large and ornate tombs and foundations of historical buildings, and many more as yet undiscovered. The museums of China's various provinces, municipalities and autonomous regions house thousands of cultural relics and works of art, among which are treasures rare in the world, displaying the long history of China and the splendid Chinese culture from different aspects. The strong, deep-rooted Chinese culture has always influenced the mentality and moral standards of the Chinese people, having developed continually in pace with the civilization. A careful study of today's Peking Opera, kunqu opera, shadow plays, calligraphy, painting, paper-cutting, and even the flower-shaped steamed buns on the kitchen range of farmers will reveal elements of traditional Chinese culture as well as replications of the art of the past.

Like other countries of venerable age, China has suffered grievous calamities. During the century and more before the 1950s, the Chinese people made unrelenting struggles for the prosperity of the country, and national independence and liberation. A large number of insightful people and revolutionaries, cherishing all kinds of dreams for a strong China, studied the ways of the West in a quest for prosperity and strength, and borrowed the revolutionary experience of foreign countries. At last, the Communist Party of China, proceeding from the reality of China, and relying on the working people, founded a brand-new country, the People's Republic of China, in 1949. Since then, the Chinese people have made persistent efforts and explorations for the grand revitalization of the Chinese nation. The Chinese people's efforts in the past two decades and more have resulted in outstanding achievements, with rapid social progress, a well-developed economy, and a modern civilization and traditional culture enhancing each other.

It is easy to have a quick look at China's past and present, but it takes time to gain a panoramic knowledge of China. The "Panoramic China" series is meant to assist readers, especially those overseas, in this respect. Each volume in the series focuses on a province, municipality or autonomous region, describing, with illustrations, the outstanding characteristics of each area from different perspectives. Through this series, the reader will acquire knowledge of the real and vivid daily life of the local people, the colorful society and the developing economy, assisted by relevant information.

Location of Beijing in the People's Republic of China

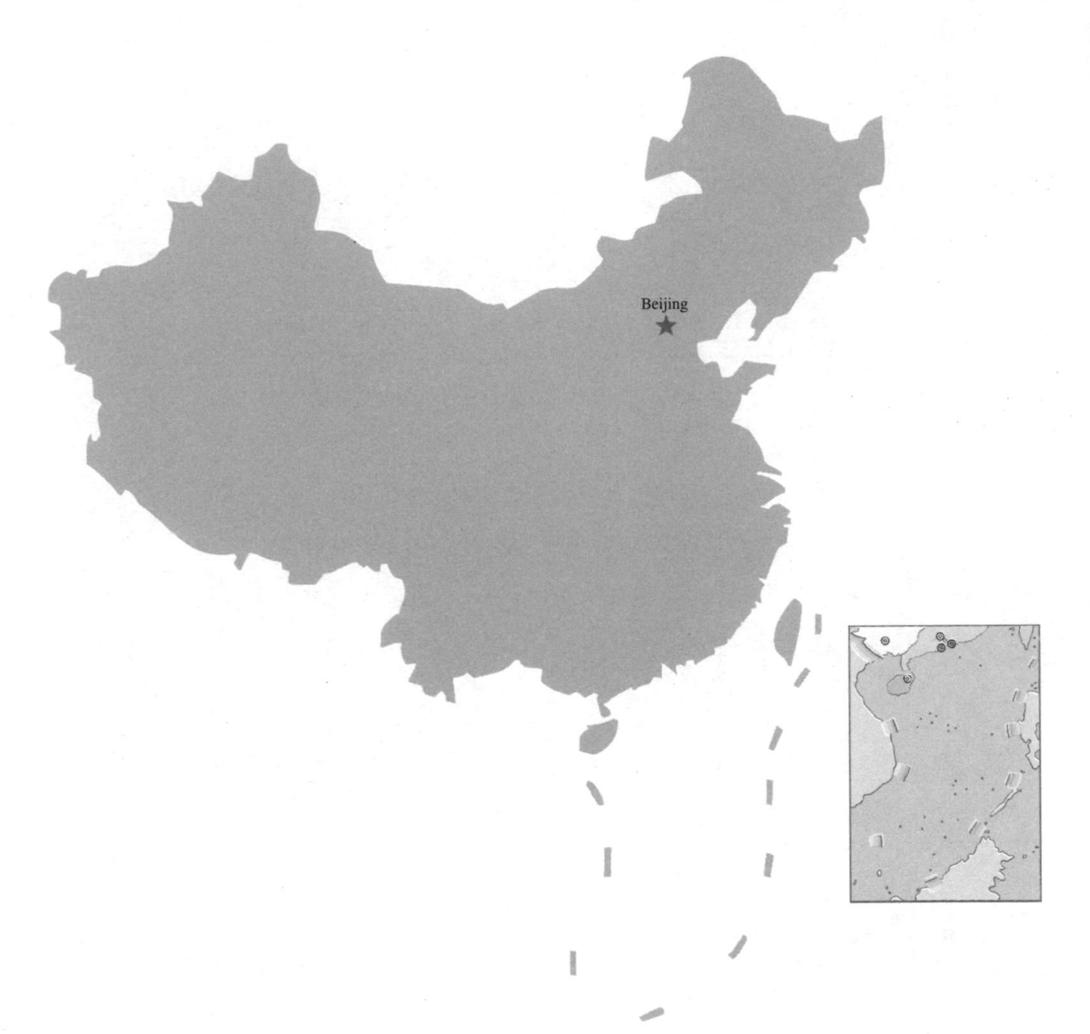

Preface

All over the world there are great cities with broad streets and impressive buildings, where historical figures have arisen and called upon their people to undertake earthshaking causes, having a far-reaching impact on their own nations and even the whole world. There are also cities with attractive scenery, long history and profound culture. Such cities attract tourists from all over the world. There are also a few cities which possess all the above-named advantages, and I'm lucky to live in one of them — Beijing.

Beijing is very old. When it was first constructed as a capital (1271, in the Yuan Dynasty), everything was planned. The outline of the city was square, which is deeply rooted in Chinese culture. There is a Chinese saying which goes "The sky is round, and the earth is a rectangle." The capital city of the Zhou Dynasty (1046-256 BC), one of the first Chinese cities, was also square-shaped. Cities in China in ancient times were usually surrounded by a city wall aligned with the east, west, south and north. A moat crossed by a drawbridge encircled the wall, which was surmounted by towers of the same height, style and decoration, except that the tower over the southern gate was usually bigger (witness the tower of the Front Gate of Beijing). No gate was set in the middle of the north side of the Beijing city wall, because it was thought that the emperor's authority would leak out if a direct passage was opened from the central north part. The emperor and his concubines lived right in the middle of the city in the area containing the main source of the city's water. A wall similar to that of the outer city wall enclosed the imperial palaces. Outside it was the royal city, where the emperor's family members and close relatives lived. Outside the royal city was another wall, outside which the common people lived. Their residences were located in even-sized square areas, with special quarters for individuals of consequence. Today, there is still one royal palace complex in Beijing, a dozen princes' residences and over 100 well-preserved courtyard houses, and numerous compounds.

Beijing remained square-shaped until the reign (1522-1567) of Emperor Jiajing of the Ming Dynasty. Fearing attack from the north, it was decided to enlarge the city by adding another outer wall. The work started in the south, instead of the direction of the military threat, but before long it had to be abandoned, because the emperor had squandered the remaining money for the project. The result was the distinctive 凸 shape of Beijing during the Ming Dynasty. The expansion of the southern part of the city attracted peddlers from their traditional trading place north of the palace complex, so that the main market settled there—the most important and conspicuous part of the city. In the Tang Dynasty (618-907) a tradition grew up of having markets on the north of the imperial palace, like those in Chang'an, capital of the Tang Dynasty, present-day Xi'an, Shaanxi Province. Here, I'd like to discuss the source of the Chinese philosophical concept of "sitting in the north and facing the south." In ancient China, as in many other countries located in the northern hemisphere, the cold and severe north was a symbol of solemnity and divinity, while the warm and indolent south was an area to be subjected to rule. The irony is that the sheer stupidity of the emperor ended up not only changing the traditional rigid Chinese philosophical rules but also in a very wise move to reshape the city of Beijing.

How has life within the city walls for so many centuries shaped the personality of the people of Beijing? The city walls are square, heavy and solid. This has made Beijing people straightforward, generous, talented, magnanimous and devoted to education, and they attach great importance to loyalty to friends. They love their city, including every brick and tile, blade of grass, tree, flower and bird. Beijing people are proud to live here generation after generation, never giving a thought to leaving this city. Such is the sense of security which the massive city walls have handed down as a legacy to the people of China's capital. Doing things without haste is a deep-rooted disposition of Beijing's people. They work, relax and entertain all at the right time, and they have so many better ways to entertain themselves than people in other parts of the country. They don't bother with things that are not their business, regarding residence "at the emperor's feet" as the ideal life. No other place could be better than here. As for foreigners, they didn't give them a thought. China was the center of the world, and Beijing was the center of China. This attitude of the people of the capital (of ignoring the outside world) led to dire consequences for China until the country opened itself up and learned to absorb others' advantages to make up for its own disadvantages.

In recent decades the population of Beijing swelled to the point at which the municipal government decided to restructure the whole city. In order to ease the congestion in the center of Beijing, large numbers of various new-style buildings were erected on the periphery of the city in all directions. These new suburbs were divided into several districts, separated by green belts. Today's Beijing has two axes—vertical and horizontal

—and two belts to the left and right of the vertical axis. The belt to the left of the vertical axis is devoted to technological development; that to the right, to cultural activities. In the past, there was only the vertical axis. Officials entered the palace to pay respects to or have an audience with the emperor by kowtowing along the vertical way. However, in modern times, communication between west and east are regarded as more important than that between south and north. In Beijing there are now horizontal "golden belts"—Chang'an Street, Ping'an Street and Liangguang Street—in addition to the two belts to the left and right of the vertical axis. The belt of technological development to the left was formed naturally in the last few decades with a little administrative regulation, and the ecological belt of cultural activities to the right developed in a similar way.

The northern part of Beijing has been expanded greatly in recent years, especially since Beijing hosted the Asian Games in 1990. Meanwhile, at the southern end of the original north-south axis, the tower of the Yongdingmen Gate Tower has been restored, and the vertical axis has been extended to Nanyuan. Chaoyang District is continuously expanding eastward, involving the development of the Tongzhou District, to which about 1.2 million people will eventually move. In the western part of Beijing, Haidian District is where most of Beijing's universities are concentrated. In addition, its modern technological research facilities have given the district the nickname "China's Silicon Valley." Behind Haidian lie the Western Hills, a scenic and recreational area. Beijing is being built with the latest concepts, combining the best of the old and the new, the elegant and the practical, the magnificent and the simple. There is something for everyone here. Beijing welcomes you to visit and participate in its construction.

More importantly, Beijing people have become more mature. Beijing is the political and cultural center of China. In the past it was thought that as long as the policies of a party and some advanced members were publicized and implemented, the country would naturally develop. Today, the trend is toward "multi-polarization," with more consideration given to the will and the interests of the majority of the people. Moreover, the old culture which rejected new things has been modified, and the principle of "developing the country by technology" has been firmly established. Nowadays, while valuing Beijing's cultural heritage, the people of this newly developing city are curious about everything foreign. They like to study new things, and adapt suitable aspects of them for the construction of Beijing.

Dear friends, I don't know if you've ever visited Beijing, but what you see in this photo album, whether it's old or new, is just a very small part of Beijing. If you come here on official business, the relevant departments of the government will warmly welcome you, arrange activities such as climbing the Great Wall, visiting the Palace Museum and tasting Beijing's famous dish, roast duck. If you visit Beijing in a private capacity, you will be able to witness the ordinary people's life, visit *hutong* (old alleys) by tricycle, and make dumplings in local homes. There have been some young foreigners who first came as tourists, but stayed in Beijing, and even set up families here, as they gradually came to understand Chinese culture and found the traditional local folk art and trade intriguing and worthwhile practicing.

Recently, a sign indicating "kilometer zero" was set up in Tian'anmen Square. This symbolizes, first of all, that Beijing is the center of China, and, second, that the past has receded, and the future starts at "zero." Every day a new sun rises! Beijing welcomes guests from all over the world!

Xu Chengbei

The Zhengyangmen Gate

The inner city of Beijing was built around the Forbidden City and the Imperial City in 1420 (the 18th year of the reign of Emperor Yongle of the Ming Dynasty - 1368-1644). Nine gates stood along the 20-km city wall. Zhengyangmen was the main gate in the center of the southern wall. The gate-tower and the arrow tower are still extant. It is popularly known as Qianmen, the "front gate," because it is situated directly in front of the Imperial City and the Forbidden City.

The gate-tower was built in 1437, the second year of the Zhengtong reign period of the Ming Dynasty. Between the gate-tower and the arrow tower there was originally a semi-circular enceinte of the city gate which was 108 m from north to south and 90 m from east to west, with four arched gates around the wall. From its construction to the early 20th century, the wall was burned down several times, then they were torn down in 1914. The next year, a German engineer was commissioned to renovate the arrow tower and redesign the surrounding streets to facilitate the flow of traffic.

The tower of the gate sits on the top of the brick city wall. It is a two-story structure with a traditional double-eaved roof. The roof is of *xieshan* style (or "combination hip-gable" style), covered with gray semi-tubular tiles fringed with green tiles on the roof edges. There are doors on all four sides of both stories. The building is divided into seven bays, called *jian*, on the south and north sides, and into three bays on the east and west sides. (A bay is the spacing between two adjacent columns.) Corridors that face the outside are on all four sides of both stories of the tower. On the east and west sides of the tower on the inner side of the wall are ramps that lead from the ground to the top of the wall. The tower is 42 m high, the highest of all gate-towers of Beijing. The arrow tower of Zhengyangmen was built in 1439, the fourth year of the reign of Ming Emperor Zheng Tong. It is a brick bastion-like structure built on top of the 12-metre high wall. The total height of the tower from the ground is 38 m. It also has the traditional double-eave *xieshan* style. There are four rows of loopholes facing towards the outside, totaling 94 in all. Originally, there were two temples in the enceinte enclosure of the city gate, one for Guan Yu, the God of War, and the other for Bodhisattva Guanyin.

Tian'anmen Square at festival time

Zhengyangmen (Qianmen, the "front gate")

The Monument to the People's Heroes in Tian'anmen Square

The *Pailou* (Decorative Archway) Outside Zhengyangmen

The *pailou* had five bays supported by six pillars, and was commonly known as the Wu Pailou (Five-bay Archway). This wooden structure is no longer extant.

Zhengyangmen today, viewed from the south

Young city people

A View of Zhonghuamen

There was a wall in front of Tian'anmen with its periphery shaped like the letter T. At the southern end of this wall was Zhonghuamen, called Damingmen (Great Ming Gate) in the Ming Dynasty and Daqingmen (Great Qing Gate) in the Qing Dynasty (1644-1911). The name was changed to Zhonghuamen after the founding of the Republic of China in 1912. The gate and the wall were torn down when Tian'anmen Square was constructed in the 1950s. This royal gate was a masonry five-bay structure with a plinth of marble. It had three arched openings and a single-eaved *xieshan* roof which was covered with the imperial yellow-glazed tiles. Formerly, as it formed an approach to Tian'anmen, the gate was guarded by soldiers, and no one was allowed to enter without permission.

A Bird's-Eye View of Zhengyangmen

The photo shows from lower left to upper right: the Arrow Gate of Zhengyangmen, Zhengyangmen (Front Gate), Zhonghuamen (China Gate), and Tian'anmen (Gate of Heavenly Peace).

The central gate of Zhengyangmen was used exclusively by the emperor, and was usually closed. The two gates on each side of the Zhengyangmen Tower were open to officials and common people alike. The square between Zhengyangmen and Zhonghuamen was called Qipanjie (Checker Board Street), which was the "downtown" district that linked the eastern and western districts. On the east side of Zhonghuamen was the district housing the six ministries of the imperial government in the Ming and Qing dynasties, while on the west side the army quarters and imperial secretariat were situated.
The district outside Zhengyangmen has been a thriving residential and commercial center ever since the Yuan Dynasty (1271-1368), and especially in the Ming and Qing dynasties. It is still a bustling commercial district today.

Taking photos in Tian’anmen Square

Celebrations in Tian’anmen Square

Tian’anmen Square at festival time

Chang'an Avenue

The Chang'an Avenue was originally 500 m long, running east-west from the Chang'an Left Gate to the Chang'an Right Gate past the front gate of the Imperial City, Chengtianmen, when it was first constructed in the reign of Ming Emperor Yongle (1403-1424). At that time, Chang'an Avenue was called Tianjie (Heavenly Street), and was closed to the public.

The avenue fell into disrepair after Qing Emperor Qianlong's reign (1736-1795) . The buildings flanking the street were damaged during the Boxer Rebellion of 1900. The avenue was rebuilt and extended in the Republican period (1912-1949), and tramlines were laid. The photo shows the *pailou* which stood on the East Chang'an Avenue in the old days.

Flag-raising ceremony in Tian'anmen Square

A panoramic view of Tian'anmen Square

The Tian'anmen Gate-Tower

Tian'anmen was the front gate of the Imperial City. It was built in 1417, the 15th year of the reign of Ming Emperor Yongle. It was formerly called Chengtianmen (the Gate for Receiving Heavenly Orders), and the name was changed to Tian'anmen in the early years of the Qing Dynasty. Tian'anmen has an elevated red terrace with five arched gate openings. On top of the terrace is an imposing palace-like structure with nine bays, double-tiered eaves, and a *xieshan* roof covered with yellow-glazed tiles. A white marble balustrade circumscribes the periphery of the structure.

In front of the gate are the five Jinshuiqiao (Golden Water Bridges), which span a 52-m-wide moat. On the right and left sides of the bridges are two huge ornamental marble columns, called *huabiao*, decorated with carved dragons.

There was a corridor with red walls leading from Tian'anmen to Zhonghuamen on the south. Along the walls of the passage were small one-story buildings called "Corridor of 1,000 Steps." There were also two small gates on the east and west sides of the wall called the Left and Right Chang'an Gate, respectively, leading to Chang'an Avenue. These gates were guarded, and only officials above a certain rank were allowed to pass through.

The grand military parade held in 1999 to mark the 50th anniversary of the founding of the People's Republic of China

The Drum Tower

The Drum Tower is situated near the northern end of the central axis of the old city of Beijing. It was built in 1420, the 18th year of the reign of Ming Emperor Yongle. It was rebuilt twice in the Qing Dynasty. The tower was built with brick and wood on a brick and stone platform. Along its length are five bays, a *xieshan* roof with gray semi-tubular tiles fringed with green-glazed tiles, and a three-tiered eave. The total height from the ground is 46.7 m, and the length and the width of the tower are respectively 34 m and 23 m. The platform has eight arched gateways at ground level: three each on the north and south sides, and one each on the east and west sides. On the second story, there are six wooden doors and windows on each of the four sides, surrounded by a veranda. The third, and top, story has no windows. A pair of marble lions sits at the southern entrance of the Drum Tower.

Drums were placed on the second floor. They were used to announce the time of day. Originally, there were 25 drums – one big and 24 small. The latter represented the 24 divisions of the solar year by the traditional Chinese calendar. The beating of the drums followed a certain pattern: Every night at seven o'clock, the big drum was struck 108 times. This was called *dinggeng* (or setting the hour). This was repeated every *geng* (two hours) until the fifth, or "dawn," *geng*, which was five o'clock in the morning. The drum had to be beaten with a certain rhythm. People still remember the ditty: "18 strokes fast, 18 strokes slow, 18 strokes neither fast nor slow." All the drums except the big one are now gone. The big one, one and a half m in diameter, is covered with a bull hide, which still bears sword marks left by Japanese soldiers during the eight-power invasion of Beijing in 1900. During the Republican period, the tower was renamed Avenge-the-Shame Tower, and in the hall were displayed models and pictures to remind the people of the atrocities committed by the invading armies.

Carved stone block supporting the pivot of a courtyard gate

A night view of Houhai (Back Lake)

The Drum Tower

The Bell Tower

About 100 m north of the Drum Tower is the two-storied Bell Tower. This is the northernmost structure on the traditional central axis of Beijing. The tower was built in 1420, the 18th year of the reign of Ming Emperor Yongle. Originally it was a wooden structure, but it was rebuilt in brick and stone in 1750, during the reign of Qing Emperor Qianlong, after a disastrous fire. The *xieshan* roof has double-tiered eaves, and is covered with black-glazed tiles with green-glazed tiles at the edges. On each of the four sides of the base is an arched gateway. On the second floor, a white marble balustrade circumscribes the periphery, and arched openings and stone windows with a lozenge motif decorate the wall. The total height of the tower is 48 m. A big bell that used to chime the passage of the hours still hangs in the second story.

The original bell was an iron one, cast in 1420, the 18th year of the reign of Emperor Yongle. It had a height of 4.2 m and a diameter of 2.4 m, and weighed 25 tons. But this bell was regarded as not being sonorous enough, and it was replaced later in Yongle's reign by a 42-ton bronze bell with a height of 5.4 m and a diameter of 3.4 m. It hangs from an octagonal wooden frame in the center of the hall on the second floor. The bell was struck 108 times twice a day – at seven in the evening and at five in the morning – signaling the times to rest and get up, respectively. On the southern side of the Bell Tower stands a stone stele bearing an inscription in Emperor Qianlong's calligraphy recording the rebuilding of the Bell Tower. On the west is the site of the Temple of the Goddess of the Golden Furnace, dedicated to the daughter of the bell caster, who is supposed to have sacrificed herself to ensure the production of a flawless bell.

The Bell Tower

Old Beijing-style courtyard house

Stone guard standing before Princess Hejing's Mansion

A panoramic view of the Bell and Drum Towers

Present-day Bell and Drum Towers

Qiniandian (Hall of Prayer for a Good Harvest) in the Temple of Heaven

The hall is located in the center of a three-tiered circular terrace called the Altar of Prayer for a Good Harvest. It was constructed in 1420, the 18th year of the reign of Ming Emperor Yongle. It was first called Daqidian (Hall of Great Prayer), and was a structure with a square plan. It was given the present round shape in the reign of Ming Emperor Jiajing (1522-1566), and renamed Daxiangdian (Hall of Great Reception).

Qiniandian is a lofty round structure with triple eaves and a cone-shaped deep-blue-glazed tile roof crowned with a gilded knob. A special feature of the construction is that the inner frame is supported by 28 massive columns and cross bars. It is 33 m high and 30 m in diameter. The four central columns, called "dragon-well pillars," are 19.2 m high and have a circumference of five arm spans. These columns represent the four seasons. They are surrounded by two concentric 12-column rings; the inner ring symbolizes the 12 months of the year, and the outer ring the 12 divisions of the day according to the ancient way of reckoning time with each division equivalent to two hours. The 24 columns together symbolize the 24 divisions of the solar year by the Chinese calendar. The 28 columns, big and small together, again symbolize the 28 heavenly constellations according to ancient Chinese astronomy. The gilded knob atop the roof symbolizes the emperor, the sole ruler under Heaven.

In the old days, the emperor used to lead the senior court officials and military officers to pray for a good harvest in the first month of the Chinese calendar every year, and for rain when there was a drought.

A reenactment of the traditional Spring Festival sacrificial ceremony at the Temple of Heaven

Hall of Prayer for Good Harvests (Qiniandian)

A reenactment of the traditional sacrificial ceremony at the Temple of Earth

The "Olympic Dragon" covering part of the Great Wall

Maurice Taylor, Dikembe Mutombo and Jim Jackson, members of the Houston Rockets, on the Great Wall

The Great Wall at Badaling

Walkers on the Great Wall

Beihai Park

Beihai (North Sea) Park is situated at the center of the Inner City. It is an outstanding example of Chinese-style landscaping, with a long history. It served as an imperial pleasure ground from the Liao Dynasty (907-1125) and through the Jin (1115-1234), Yuan, Ming, and Qing dynasties until it was opened to the public in 1922 as a park.

In the middle of the 11th century, Beihai was a temporary imperial palace northeast of the secondary capital Yanjing of the Liao Dynasty (the Liao capital was in present-day Inner Mongolia). In the 12th century, during the Jin Dynasty, a hill was piled up by dredging the mud from the lake, and rockery was transported from the imperial gardens of the Northern Song Dynasty (960-1127) in Bianliang (now called Kaifeng, in Henan Province) and more palace halls were built on what is now called Jade Islet. In the 13th century, Kublai Khan (r. 1260-1294), the first emperor of the Yuan Dynasty, built his capital around the garden, and carried out large-scale reconstruction of Jade Islet, including a grand expansion of Guanghan Palace. The palace, unfortunately, was destroyed by an earthquake 300 years later. The Ming and Qing dynasties saw further expansions of the garden. In 1651, the White Dagoba, a Tibetan-style Buddhist tower, was constructed there at the suggestion of a leading Tibetan lama by the name of Nomhan. Qing Emperor Shunzhi agreed to the project as a gesture of devotion to the Buddhist faith and a desire for unity among China's ethnic groups.

In 1741, Emperor Qianlong ordered a large-scale renovation of the garden. An account of the construction and a description of the scenic spots in the garden were inscribed on separate stone steles placed at the foot of the hill on which the White Dagoba stands.

A panoramic view of Beihai Park (North Sea Lake)

The Nine-dragon Screen in Beihai Park

Taihedian (Hall of Supreme Harmony)

The Forbidden City viewed from Coal Hill in Jingshan Park

Suzhou Market Street in the Summer Palace

The Tower of Buddhist Incense in the Summer Palace

The Nine-dragon Amusement Park near the Ming Tombs

The Sacred Way at the Eastern Qing Tombs

Yonghegong (Lamasery of Harmony and Peace)

Yonghegong, popularly known as the Lama Temple, is the biggest and best-preserved place of worship of Tibetan Buddhism in Beijing. Covering an area of 66,400 sq m, the lamasery is considered to be very well designed as it mingles the opulence of a magnificent palace and the solemnity of place for devotion in one complex.

The original site of the lamasery was a residential area for Ming Dynasty eunuchs. In 1694, Qing Emperor Kangxi built a mansion for his fourth son, who later ascended the throne as Emperor Yongzheng (r. 1723-1735). Yongzheng devoted half of the site to the construction of a lamasery and reserved the other half for a temporary palace for himself. After his death, his son Emperor Qianlong gave over the whole area to the lamasery, and also used it as the center of administration for Tibetan Buddhist affairs.

Architecturally, Yonghegong combines Han, Manchu, Mongolian, and Tibetan styles. The complex includes five main shrines with adjoining halls and other buildings arranged around seven courtyards. The monastery houses a rich collection of Buddhist and other cultural relics. The photo shows the halls and *pailou* in the southernmost courtyard, which was built in 1744, in the Qing Dynasty.

Lamas in Yonghegong (Lamasery of Harmony and Peace)

The giant statue of Buddha in Wanfuge (Pavilion of Every Happiness)

The Chongwenmen Gate-Tower

There were three gates in the southern part of the city wall of the Inner City: Zhengyangmen in the middle, Xuanwumen in the west and Chongwenmen in the east. In the Yuan Dynasty (1271-1368), when Beijing, then called Dadu, was the capital, Chongwenmen was called Wenmingmen, and was also popularly known as Hadamen. This is noted in the *Annals of Xijin* (Xijin was the former name of Beijing in the Liao Dynasty when it was still a prefecture): "Wenmingmen is also called Hadamen, because Prince Hada's mansion was inside the gate." The name Wenmingmen was still used in the early Ming Dynasty, but it was changed later to Chongwenmen, because a temple to Confucius and the Literary Academy were nearby. The two characters "chong" and "wen" mean "respect for culture and education." Sometimes Chongwenmen is translated as Gate of Exalted Literature.

The gate-tower was rebuilt in 1436, the first year of the reign of Ming Emperor Zhengtong. It has a *xieshan* roof with three tiers of sweeping eaves covered with gray semi-tubular tiles lined with green-glazed tiles on the fringes. The height of the tower is 33-37 m, the width from east to west is 36-37 m, and it is divided into five *jian* (bays). The depth is 19-23 m.

The photo shows the front view of Chongwenmen.

Bronze lions, guarding the entrance of many parks, have witnessed great changes in the capital.

The Dongzhimen Gate-Tower

Of the two gates in the eastern part of the city wall of the Inner City, the southern one was named Chaoyangmen, and the northern one, Dongzhimen. The latter name has been used since the Ming Dynasty; it was called Chongrenmen when it was constructed in the Yuan Dynasty. The name "Dongzhi" refers to a saying: "Teach the people as far as the eastern seas." The Dongzhimen gate-tower was a structure of five bays, with a *xieshan* roof, and gray semi-tubular tiles fringed with green-glazed tiles. It had three tiers of eaves, and was 33 m high, 36-39 m wide and 19-23 m deep.

Dongzhimen's Arrow Tower was a seven-bay structure with four rows of loopholes each on three sides, totaling 82 in all. On the back of the tower there were five additional bays and three doors. It had two-tier eaves with a *xieshan* roof, and semi-tubular gray tiles fringed with green-glazed tiles. The bastion-like structure had a total height of 30-32 m. The Arrow Tower did not have gate openings directly below it.

Lockgates were installed at the left and right sides of the enceinte of the city gate for the flow of traffic. Lockgate-towers above the lockgates held up the heavy gates. On the outside of these lockgate-towers were two rows of loopholes, 12 in all. A portcullis weighing 500 kilograms was installed in the lockgate.

Dongzhimen was bombarded by the British and French forces during the Second Opium War (1860), and again in 1900 by troops of the eight invading powers. The Dongzhimen enceinte wall was torn down in 1915 to make way for railroad construction. In 1927, the Arrow Tower was torn down.

The photo shows the Dongzhimen gate-tower.

Newlyweds posing before a cathedral

Interior of a traditional Beijing courtyard house

New houses in traditional style are replacing the old, dilapidated ones in Beijing's famous winding lanes (*hutong*).

The Chaoyangmen Gate-Tower

Chaoyangmen was located in the eastern part of the city wall of the Inner City, south of Dongzhimen. The two characters "chao" and "yang" mean "welcoming guests at sunrise." The gate did not escape bombardment by the British and French forces in 1860 or the forces of the eight powers in 1900. Its enceinte enclosure was torn down in 1915, and the rest of the gate-tower was demolished in the 1960s.

To the southeast of Chaoyangmen is the Tonghui River, which was part of the waterway by which grain was transported from South China to the capital. There were a number of warehouses for storing grain inside Chaoyangmen, while the piers for unloading it were outside the city wall, so carts loaded with grain regularly passed through Chaoyangmen.

Yuan Dynasty Wall Relic Park

Beijing at dusk

The development of a three-dimensional round-the-city road network played an important role in Beijing's successful bid for the 2008 Olympic Games.

The Caihuying Flyover

The Fuchengmen Gate-Tower

Fuchengmen was located in the western part of the city wall of the Inner City, corresponding to Chaoyangmen in the east. The two characters "fu" and "cheng" mean "thriving and peaceful." The gate-tower and its arrow tower were both demolished in the 1960s.

The photo shows the gate-tower as seen from a distance.

Street decorations in preparation for National Day

Dongsi Shitiao (East Four Tenth Lane)

The Xizhimen Flyover at night

The Southeastern Corner-Tower of the Inner City

This tower is situated southeast of the present Beijing Railway Station. It was built in 1437, the second year of the reign of Ming Emperor Zhengtong, together with the nine gate-towers of the Inner City. It is the only remaining corner-tower of Beijing's city wall.

It was built on a terrace of 1,200 sq m formed by an extension at the top of the junction of the east and south city walls. The tower itself is 17 m high and it stands 29 m from the ground. The tower is L-shaped, with double-tier eaves and a *xieshan* roof. There are some bays extending from the back of the tower, where two doors are located. The roof is covered with gray semi-tubular tiles fringed with green-glazed tiles. There are 144 loopholes in four rows on the two front sides.

A side view of the Southeastern Corner-tower of the Inner City.

Mass sports performance

The Tianningsi (Temple of Heavenly Peace) Flyover

A *hutong* (old narrow alleys) tour

Arrow Tower of Andingmen

Andingmen (Gate of Peace and Stability) was the gate in the eastern side of the northern part of the wall of the Inner City. In the Yuan Dynasty it was called Anzhenmen. The name Andingmen and the name of the other gate —Deshengmen (Gate of Moral Victory) in the western side of the northern wall, respectively refer to "civil officials manage state affairs in peacetime" and "military officers report victories on the battlefield and return triumphant." The arrow tower of Andingmen had the same shape as the other arrow towers of the Inner City. The enceinte of the city gate was torn down in 1915.

Deshengmen (Gate of Moral Victory)

Tian'anmen Square decorated for a festival

Newly built residential area

Fangzhuang Yuting Flyover

The Yongdingmen Gate-Tower

There were three gates in the southern wall of Beijing's Outer City: Zuo'anmen was on the east, You'anmen on the right, and Yongdingmen was the central gate. Yongdingmen (Gate of Eternal Stability) marked the southern starting point of the major north-south axis of Beijing's city plan.

Yongdingmen (Gate of Eternal Stability) after reconstruction

The largest greening project in the city, near Yongdingmen

Most Beijingers live in modern buildings now.

The View at Dongbianmen

Dongbianmen (Eastern Informal Gate) was built in the reign (1522-1567) of Ming Emperor Jiajing, together with the Outer City, located at its northeast corner. The original moat between Chongwenmen and Dongbianmen was outside the wall of the Inner City. But when the Outer City was built more than 100 years later, the moat was located inside the wall of the Outer City. It was the main outlet for the water of the Three Lakes and the Imperial River of the Forbidden City.

The moat was quite wide, with plenty of water flowing through it. Weeping willows flanked the two banks, and flocks of white ducks sported there.

Laptops and cars have become necessary parts of Beijing people's lives.

The old city proper around Chongwenmen

Beijing is speeding up its modernization drive.

The Arrow Tower of You'anmen

The You'anmen (Right Gate of Peace) gate-tower was a single-eaved structure of three bays. It had a *xieshan* roof covered with gray semi-tubular tiles. A door opened on each of the four sides of the tower. It was 15 m high, 19 m wide and 6 m deep.

The arrow tower of You'anmen was also a single-eaved structure of three bays, *xieshan* roof and gray tiles. On the three outer sides there were 26 loopholes. An arched gateway was directly below the arrow tower facing the main gate-tower. The total height of the arrow tower from the ground was 15 m, the width was 13 m, and the depth was 7.5 m.

Billboards are a common sight.

Fangzhuang residential area

Siyuan Flyover

The Dongsi *Pailou* (The Four Eastern Decorated Archways)

When Beijing was reconstructed in the reign of Ming Emperor Yongle, the Four Eastern and Four Western Decorated Archways (each group of archways facing the four directions) were built at the east and west crossroads, respectively, three *li* from Shenwumen (Gate of Divine Might), the north gate of the Forbidden City. These wooden *pailou* had the same design: three bays, four columns and a tiled roof. The wooden pillars rested on stone pedestals. They each bore an inscription near the top. Those facing north and south were inscribed with the characters "Dashijie" (big thoroughfare), and those facing east and west were inscribed with the characters "Lüren" (practice benevolence) and "Xingyi" (perform righteousness).

The photo shows one of the Four Eastern Archways.

White Dagoba Temple and surroundings

Streetside cafe

Former Residence of Lu Xun

The Xisi *Pailou* (The Four Western Decorated Archways)

Strolling at dusk by Houhai (Rear Lake)

Typical *hutong* scene

Lovers

The Dongdan *Pailou* (The Eastern Single Decorated Archway)

At the eastern and western ends of Chang'an Avenue there was a single archway called respectively the Dongdan *Pailou* and the Xidan *Pailou*. They were constructed at the same time as the Four Eastern and Four Western Archways, and had a similar shape. The inscription on the western archway was originally "Zhanyun" (watching the clouds) and that on the eastern archway was "Jiuyue" (moving towards the moon). In 1916, these inscriptions were changed to "Qingyun" (propitious cloud) and "Jingxing" (auspicious star), respectively. The photo shows the Eastern Single Archway after the change of names.

Xidan Culture Square

The *Pailou* at the Two Ends of Beihai Bridge

The big bridge that separates Beihai (North Sea) and Zhonghai (Central Sea) is called the Golden Tortoise Jade Rainbow Bridge, as mentioned in a previous section. The name derives from the *pailou* which once stood at each end of the bridge. The western *pailou* was inscribed with the characters "Jin'ao" (golden tortoise), and the eastern *pailou* with the characters "Yudong" (jade rainbow). The photo shows the Jin'ao *Pailou*.

A visitor takes part in a Chinese calligraphy competition.

Making traditional sugar figurines

Jingshan Park at dusk

The Southern Cathedral

The Southern Cathedral was constructed inside the Xuanwumen Gate, in the southern part of Beijing. It is the oldest Catholic church in Beijing. Built in 1605, in the 33rd year of the reign of Ming Emperor Wanli, by the Italian Jesuit priest Matteo Ricci, it was rebuilt by the German Jesuit priest Johann Adam Schall von Bell, in the seventh year (1651) of the reign of Qing Emperor Shunzhi. The building was renovated in 1712, 1776 and 1904.

The cathedral is a fine example of the Gothic style, with carved bricks and stained glass windows and doors. The pulpit and altar are elaborately decorated.

The picture shows the façade of the church in 1904, shortly after it was last renovated.

Ready for the newlyweds

Dongjiaomin Xiang

Dongjiaomin Xiang (East Dealing-with-the-People Lane) runs parallel to and south of Chang'an Avenue. It stretches from Qianmen (Front Gate) eastward to Chongwenmennei Street, crossing many north-south streets. During the Ming and Qing dynasties, institutions for managing relations with Western nations and with ethnic minorities living on China's borders were located here. In the early 20th century, the Eight Allied Powers (Britain, the United States, Germany, Japan, Russia, France, Italy and Austria) invaded Beijing and made this area the legation section. There they built embassies, barracks, hospitals, banks, churches and office buildings for foreign business firms. The picture shows the lane in that period.

Unusual teahouse decoration

After rain

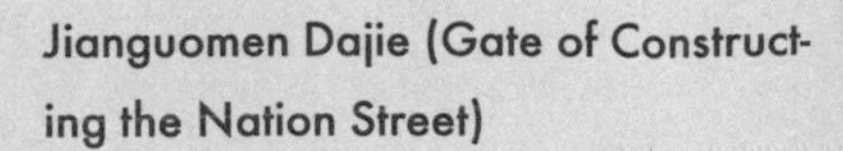

Jianguomen Dajie (Gate of Constructing the Nation Street)

The Beijing Union Medical College and Its Hospital

This college, more popularly known by its acronym of PUMC, is located on Shuaifuyuan Street. It was originally the mansion of Prince Yu, the 15th son of Nurhachi, the founder of the Qing Dynasty. The mansion was sold to the Rockefeller Foundation in 1916 by the Republican government. The new owners then dismantled the original buildings and designed and constructed a complex equipped with the latest technical appliances and modern conveniences for teaching medicine, together with a hospital, while retaining the traditional Chinese style and façade on the outside. The sweeping roof was covered with green tiles and the walls were of finely ground bricks. It was an architectural achievement.

PUMC attained international fame as a world-class medical college, and has trained a large number of doctors and medical scholars. The college and the hospital are still in operation, and are held in great esteem.

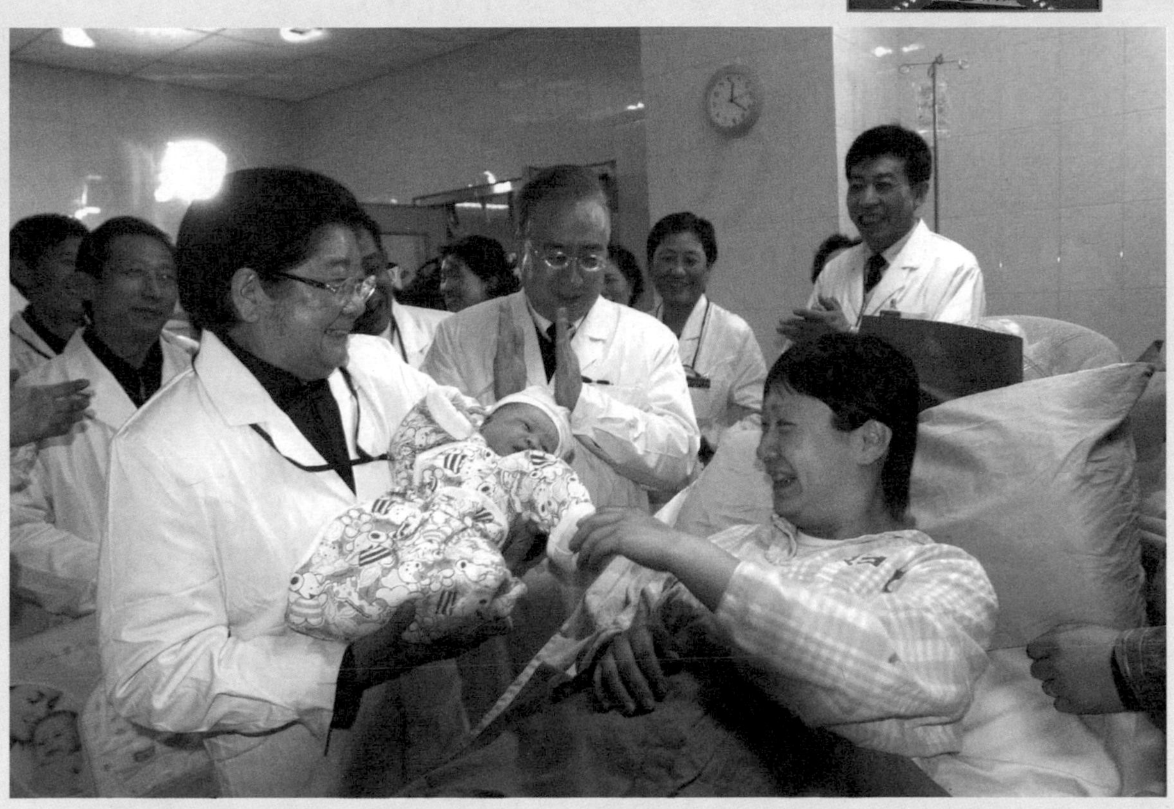

China's 1.3 billionth citizen came into the world at 0:02 am on January 6, 2005, at the Beijing Maternity Hospital.

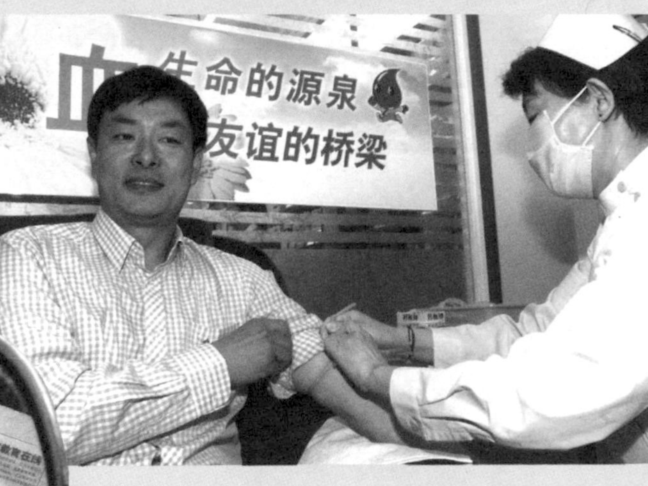

Blood donation

The media gave timely information during the SARS epidemic in 2003.

Hotel de Wagon-Lits

Located on the eastern side of the southern end of Yuheqiao Street, this building occupied one block of the street from Dongjiaomin Xiang southward to the former Qianmen Railway Station. It was once the biggest Western-style building in Beijing. Many conferences and treaties of historical importance were held or signed here in the 19th and 20th centuries.

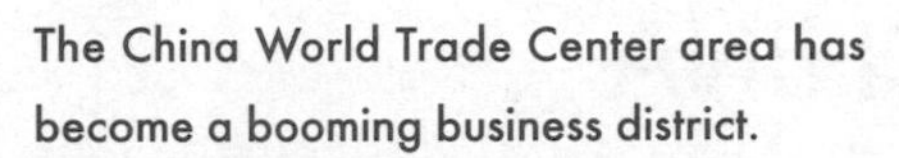

The China World Trade Center area has become a booming business district.

East Lake Villas residential complex

The Glazed Archway of Guozijian

Guozijian (Imperial Academy) was the highest educational institution in the country in the Yuan, Ming and Qing dynasties. The academy was first built in the Yuan Dynasty on the east side of the Confucius Temple, in conformity with the traditional Chinese architectural rule of temple to the left and academy to the right.

The glazed archway shown in the photo stands behind the front gate. The inscription on the north and south sides on the lintel of the archway was written by Emperor Qianlong in his own calligraphy, prescribing the nature and goal of the academy.

The academy was renovated in the Qianlong period, in the style of a Confucian Temple. The color of the glazed roof tiles was then changed to yellow, which was the color reserved for the emperor. Qianlong ordered the texts of the Thirteen Classics of Confucianism to be inscribed on steles, which were then erected in the six halls on the east and west sides of the academy. This set of steles is the only complete set of the thirteen classical works inscribed on stone.

The 10th China International Education Exhibition Tour opened in Beijing on February 26th, 2005. The picture shows the display counter of a bank that offers financial services to Chinese overseas students.

Archway of Guozijian (Imperial College)

Graduation photo

Tsinghua School

Tsinghua School, the predecessor of Tsinghua University, is a Western-style building with an octagonal plan. The four characters of the name of the school were inscribed above the front gate. It was built in 1909, the first year of the reign of Xuantong, the last Qing emperor, on the site of the former Qing Dynasty imperial garden known as Xichunyuan. Tsinghua School went into formal operation in 1911. After continued expansion, it became Tsinghua University in 1928.

A corner of Tsinghua University

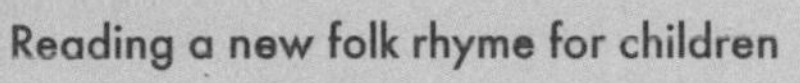

Reading a new folk rhyme for children

Yenching University

In the early years of the Republic, Yenching University was built on the site of Shaoyuan, a beautiful landscape garden originally owned by the Ming painter and calligrapher Mi Wanzhong. The general layout of the campus and the buildings was designed by American architects. All the buildings display the characteristics of traditional Chinese architecture, with sweeping roofs and red pillars. From the very beginning, they were equipped with modern conveniences such as central heating, plumbing and electric lighting. The buildings harmonized so well with the beautiful garden landscape that some American professors considered the Yenching campus as the most beautiful of its kind in the world.

The pair of carved marble pillars in the photo was originally placed in front of the Anyou Palace of the Yuanmingyuan Garden, the so-called Old Summer Palace which was burned down by the British and French armies in 1860. The intricately carved stone pillars are representative works of art of the mid-Qing period.

Before the 1950s, Yenching had three colleges, 18 departments and a graduate school. In 1952, Peking University (Beida), which was located at Shatan in the city proper, moved to the Yenching campus. Yenching University, together with some other colleges, was then amalgamated with Beida.

Weiming Lake of Peking University

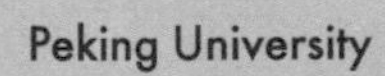
Peking University

The Beijing Library

The Beijing Library has a long history and a huge collection of books. This world-famous library was originally called Capital Library when it was founded in the first year of the reign (1909-1911) of the last Qing emperor, Xuantong. The library site was located on the north bank of Houhai, in the Guanghua Temple. Its collection included part of the imperial collections of books of Song, Yuan, Ming and Qing dynasties as well as the private collections of the scholars Yao Jinyuan of Gui'an and Xu Naichang of Nanling. When it was founded, it had 10,000 volumes, including many Buddhist sutras from the Mogao Caves of Dunhuang, the *Yongle Encyclopedia* of the Ming Dynasty and *The Complete Library of the Four Branches of Literature* compiled in the Qing Dynasty.

The library moved to an old dormitory of the Imperial Academy, known as Guozijian, in June 1915, and moved again to Jurentang in Zhongnanhai (Central and South Lake) late in 1928, with the name of the library changed to the National Library of Beiping. It amalgamated with the Beihai Library of Beiping the following year and the construction of a new set of buildings was started on Wenjin Street. The construction of the new library was completed in 1931, and it was opened to the public on July 1, 1931. The main buildings of the new library were in traditional palace style, but they had all the conveniences of a modern library. The complex fitted very well with neighboring Beihai Park and Zhonghai.

Children's section of a bookshop

Capital Library

The National Library of China

The Ancient Observatory

The Beijing Ancient Observatory is located to the southwest of Jianguomen Gate. With a history of over 500 years, it was the center of astronomical observation in the Ming and Qing dynasties. Built in the reign (1436-1449) of Ming Emperor Zhengtong, it was first called "The Terrace for Observing the Stars." The astronomical instruments used were copied from Yuan Dynasty models. In the reign (1628-1644) of Ming Emperor Chongzhen, a new set of instruments was made by Xu Guangqi and others, and a big advance was made in astronomical observation. The European system of astronomical measurement was introduced in the Kangxi period (1662-1722), and at the same time new types of instruments were designed and made by the Belgian Jesuit priest Father Verbiest.

The bronze astronomical instruments on display at the observatory are representative works of science and technology of the Qing period.

Wang Qishan, mayor of Beijing, explains the future city layout to representatives of the National People's Congress (NPC).

Wangfujing Street

Jianguomen (Gate of Constructing the Nation)

Street poster: "Youthful CBD (Central Business District)"

Poster put out by the Beijing Organizing Committee for the XXIX Olympiad

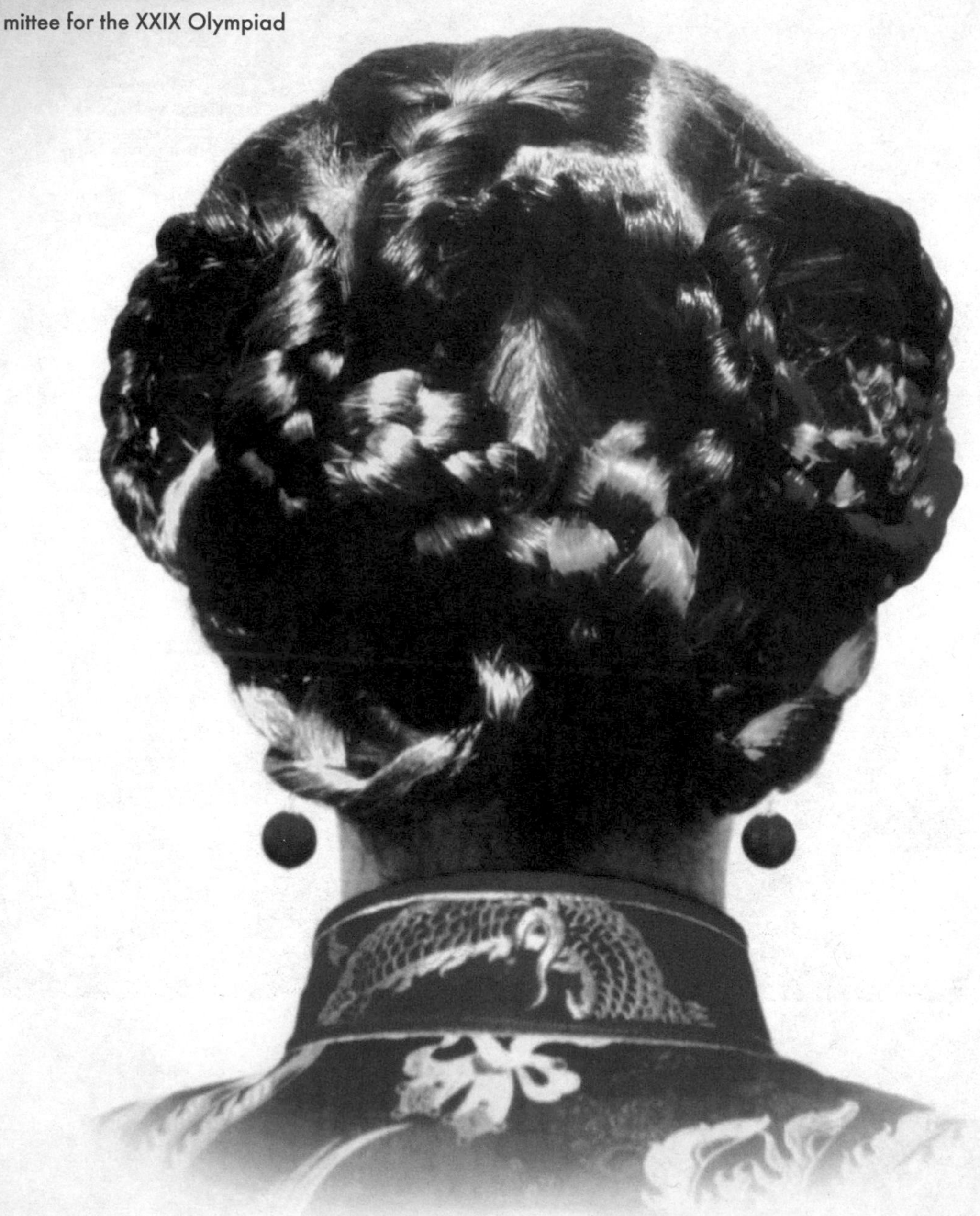

Basketball star Yao Ming ignites the ceremonial cauldron with the 2004 Athens Olympic torch.

2004 Athens Olympic torch relay activity in Beijing

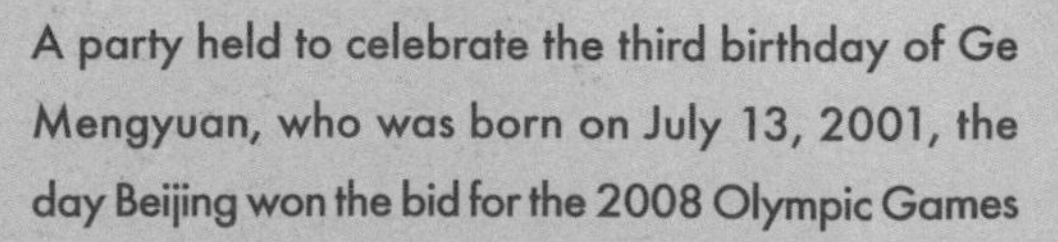

A party held to celebrate the third birthday of Ge Mengyuan, who was born on July 13, 2001, the day Beijing won the bid for the 2008 Olympic Games

Wang Qishan, mayor of Beijing, receives the Olympic flag at the closing ceremony of the 2004 Athens Olympic Games.

Poster in the office of the Beijing Organizing Committee for the XXIX Olympiad

Dough figurines with an Olympic theme

To the east of Tian'anmen Square stands the countdown board for the Beijing 2008 Olympic Games.

Celebration at the Hall of Prayer for Good Harvests at the Temple of Heaven on the occasion of the issuing of the emblem of the 2008 Beijing Olympics

The Liulichang Book Stores

To the southwest of Zhengyangmen (Front Gate), there is a market area called Liulichang, which was already a bustling commercial district in the early years of the Qing Dynasty. In the reign of Emperor Kangxi, officials and candidates attending the imperial examinations liked to stroll through the fair held at the nearby Temple of the God of Earth and peruse the book stores and book stalls that lined the street. The market became even more thriving in the 18th century. A good supply of books and even rare editions could usually be found on the book shelves. Scholars and bookworms alike frequented the street. In the 20th century the two most famous book stores were Wuliuju (Five-Willow Book Store) and Wencuitang (Hall Where Scholars Assemble).

The 6th Book Fair held in Ditan (Altar of Earth) Park in October 2004

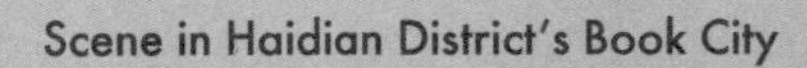

Scene in Haidian District's Book City

Beijing International Book Fair

Dashalan

Dashalan (Great Fence) has been a thriving shopping center in Beijing since the 15th century. Originally, called the Fourth Langfang Lane, its name was changed to Dashalan when barriers, in the form of fences, were set up at either end of the lane for security purposes, which were closed as soon as the curfew came into effect. The photo shows the western end of the lane. We still can see the gate of the fence in the picture.

There were two reasons why Dashalan was a thriving market for so long. First, many shops selling all kinds of goods, including a number of famous ones, were situated in this lane. They included Tongrentang Drug Store, Mafuyuan Hatter, Ruifuxiang Silk and Leather Store, Neiliansheng Shoe Store, Tianhuizhai Tobacco Store and Changhehou Wool Store, some of which had been established as early as in the 17th century. Second, many famous actors performed in the theaters in Dashalan, such as Qingleyuan, Sanqingyuan, Guangheyuan, Tongleyuan and Guangdeyuan. These theaters drew crowds of people, especially ranking officials and wealthy merchants.

In the old days, when there was a festival of some sort, palace lanterns were hung in front of every store, thus forming a miniature lantern festival which gradually became quite famous.

Famous old shops in Dashalan and Qianmen Dajie (Front Gate Avenue)

The Liulichang Curio Shops

Venders of curios, paintings, works of calligraphy, and the "four treasures" of the study, viz: writing paper, ink slab, writing brush and ink stone, also thrived in the Liulichang area in the 18th century. Especially after the looting of the Old Summer Palace, Yuanmingyuan, by foreign troops in 1860, many cultural relics were lost, only to be collected later by the common people. Along with the collapse of the Qing Empire, many aristocratic families were ruined, and had to sell their art collections.

All this made the curio business thrive. In the early 20th century, there were over 100 curio shops in Liulichang. Some curio merchants even established purchasing agents in other big cities, making Liulichang a market that covered the whole country. After years of apprenticeship and training, many such merchants became experts in the appraisal of Chinese cultural relics, winning the admiration of historians and archaeologists.

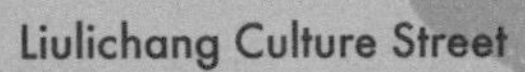

Liulichang Culture Street

Wenshengzhai Studio

This store was located on the First Lane of Langfang Street. It sold palace lanterns, gauze lanterns, and silk lanterns in various shapes. It also sold paper fans carrying brush-and-ink paintings.

Secondhand goods market

Choosing Chinese calligraphy at an art-work market

Guanyin Temple Street

A busy street outside Zhengyangmen (Front Gate)

Appraising cultural relics excavated in Beijing

Restoring an imperial robe

2004 Rongbaozhai Autumn Artwork Auction

Yihechang Drapery Store

Located outside Zhengyangmen, this store did both wholesale and retail business, selling both hand- and machine-woven cloth famous for its fine yarn since the early 20th century. Dealers from Inner Mongolia, and Gansu and Shanxi provinces used to come here to buy merchandise to take back home to sell.

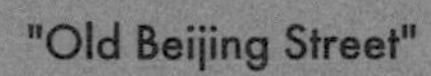
"Old Beijing Street"

Deyuancheng Cotton Store

Located outside Zhengyangmen, this store displayed a unique shop sign consisting of a large ball of cotton tied up with red ribbons.

Fashion show

Jinyuan Time Shopping Center, the largest mall in Asia

Show window

A Street Scene Outside Zhengyangmen

The photo shows the street lined with stores. The farthest from the viewer is a Chinese medicine store. The one in the middle sold assorted goods such as straw hats and basins. The nearest one is Shengtaihe Tea Store, which bought its stock directly from the tea-producing areas in the provinces of Anhui, Zhejiang and Fujian.

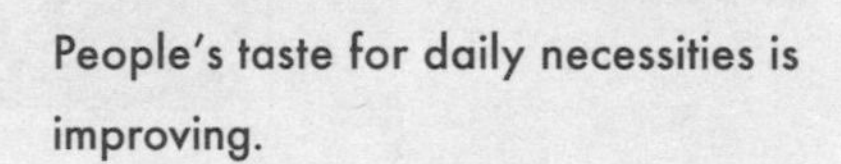

People's taste for daily necessities is improving.

Tobacco Store

In Beijing tobacco stores, samples were displayed for customers to sample. The photo shows a customer trying the tobacco.

There were also tobacco and cigarette venders and stalls on the street.

Wine tasting salon

American fast food outlets have proliferated in Beijing.

Stores That Sold Funeral Objects

The shop sign was usually a flower basket made of paper, or just a plain paper wreath. A more elaborate one was a paper carriage. In the old days, it was believed that the deceased needed everyday objects in the afterlife. And so household utilities, clothing, and even horses and carriages, all made of paper and wood, were carried in the funeral procession, and ceremoniously burned by the graveside. Naturally, there were shops which specialized in this type of merchandise.

Eye-catching statues decorating traditional restaurants

The Tianqiao Market

Tianqiao has a history of 600 years as a bustling market place. There used to be a stone bridge here over which the Ming and Qing emperors used to pass on their way to sacrifice at the nearby Temple of Heaven, hence the name Tianqiao (Heavenly Bridge).

Tianqiao Market was formally set up in 1914 by a group of merchants, who constructed seven lanes lined with stalls. By 1930, there were 773 registered stalls and restaurants, as well as a cinema. This market catered mostly to local people of the lower classes.

Shopping centers are becoming more and more modern.

New Xiushui Building, opened March 19, 2005.

Beijing Urban-Rural Trading Center

Dongxinglou Restaurant

Located on a busy street outside Donghuamen (East China Gate), Dongxinglou was the foremost among the eight big restaurants that had a name terminating with *lou*. It was noted for its freshwater fish dishes. Most of the leading restaurants in Beijing were owned by people from Shandong Province, who had specialized in this trade since the mid-17th century.

Another kind of restaurant, also owned by Shandong people, only served banquets for rich people. Usually the banquets were for a birthday party or a wedding. There were many restaurants of this kind, and their names all ended with *tang* (meaning "hall"). Examples are Fushoutang in Goldfish Lane, Qingshoutang near the Xisi *Pailou* and Tianshoutang outside Zhengyangmen.

As these restaurants were exclusive and expensive, another type of restaurant with names ending in *ju* (meaning "house") sprang up to serve the middle class. There were eight famous restaurants with names with this terminal. Their selling point was special dishes. Tongheju at Xisi, with a history of 80 years, and Shaguoju also at Xisi, with a history of 200 years, are two that are still operating. Counted among the well-established restaurants in the capital, having several branches each, are Fengzeyuan with its "new Beijing dishes" and Quanjude and Bianyifang with their roast duck.

More people from other parts of China came to Beijing in the 20th century, and restaurants serving dishes from all over the country sprang up. So the restaurants in Beijing became much more diversified.

Mutton hotpot is a Beijing favorite.

Beijing is famous for its roast duck

An elegant restaurant

There are restaurants of all styles and cuisines in Beijing.

Various kinds of traditional lanterns

Beijing West Railway Station

Camel Caravans

As late as the 1940s the transport of coal, lime and timber from the western mountainous areas into Beijing was mostly done by camel train. In the summer, the weather was considered to be too hot for the camels, which were then driven to pastures north of the Great Wall. The camel raisers mostly lived in the western suburb of Mentougou or in the southern suburb of Dahuichang.

Camel caravans were replaced by trucks in the 1940s, and camels gradually disappeared from the streets of Beijing.

TV entertainment in a bus

Beijing's subway is expanding rapidly.

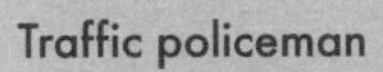

Traffic policeman

The new terminal of Beijing Capital International Airport

View of the Beijing subway system

A Brief Respite after Long Trudge

After the goods they carried had been unloaded, the camels had to be watered.

Sewage treatment plant

The Xiaoyue River flows through the northeast part of the city.

Boating on Shichahai Lake

Mule Carts

Mule carts were Beijing's main means of public transportation before the appearance of rickshaws in the late 19th century. The awning was made of blue cloth fringed with dark satin, the interior was decorated with satin of different colors, and the ceiling was white. There was a glass window on each side. Large and luxurious mule carts were for the rich and aristocratic, and small and utilitarian ones for ordinary people, like the one in the picture. Beijing's mule carts were finely crafted, being considered the best in the country.

Young men of rich families liked to drive their own mule carts, and the streets around Tianqiao were notorious for their reckless driving and racing.

Production Lines at Beijing Hyundai Motor Co.

Mule Sedans

A sedan chair slung between two mules was a common means of transportation for long journeys in the Beijing area up to the early 20th century.

Motor show

View of the 8th Beijing International Automotive Industry Exhibition (Auto China 2004)

Memorial Ceremony for Confucius

The Confucius Temple, located on Guozijian Street within Andingmen (Gate of Stability), is the second-largest Confucius Temple in China. A solemn memorial ceremony for Confucius was held twice a year, in spring and autumn, during the Qing Dynasty and into the Republican period. The ceremony started at three o'clock in the morning, with the beating of drums and the ringing of bells. After that came the playing of music, ceremonial bowing, and welcoming and sending off of the spirits of the sage, which lasted until dawn. The photo shows a scene from one of the ceremonies held in the Republican era.

Statue of Confucius in front of the Gate of Great Achievements (Dachengmen) of the Confucius Temple

Central building of the Confucius Temple, where the Qing emperors gave lectures

Making a rubbing of an ancient carving of Confucius

Performance of ancient music for worshipping Confucius

The Buzha Dance

Among the numerous Buddhist rituals and activities held at Yonghegong(Lamasery of Harmony and Peace), is the Buzha, or "Ghost Beating Dance." The climax of the dance is the cutting off of the heads of effigies of ghosts, signifying the exorcism of evil spirits.

The Buzha or Ghost Beating Dance, held annually in Yonghegong

徐悲鸿

Beijing people will never forget great men like Guo Shoujing, Li Dazhao, Mao Zedong, Lao She, Mei Lanfang....

Learning to Read and Write

In the early years of the 20th century when the modern schooling system had not yet been properly established, many families, including some who were not well-off, had their children tutored by private teachers.

At a kindergarten

A long painting scroll drawn by 200 kindergarten pupils to welcome the 2008 Beijing Olympics

Electronic publications

Happy rural children at festival time

A Young Peddler

This peddler is selling flower baskets made of paper. He has with him a pet bird.

A cool show in Xidan Culture Square

Red flags flutter in the breeze at the Great Hall of the People, and children hold national flags in Tian'anmen Square to welcome the opening of the NPC and CPPCC conferences.

Ren Yi, a fifth-grade pupil of Kangleli Primary School in Xuanwu District, published a written proposal on the Internet advocating the establishment of a Children's Environmental Protection Festival. More than 200,000 people at home and abroad signed their names in support of her suggestion.

Stalls Selling Second-Hand Clothing

Most stalls that sold second-hand clothing in Beijing were concentrated at Tianqiao, Sanguan Temple near Dongsi, and Dongdashi. People with meager means would select what they wanted here. The sellers would shout impromptu doggerel, sometimes two of them shouting alternately, to introduce their goods, which would usually draw a big crowd.

Robot display in the China Science & Technology Museum

Robots playing Chinese chess

A Traditional Store

A typical frontage of a traditional store with exquisitely carved wooden boards and balustrades over the roof was designed to make the store look elegant and attractive. A cloth awning was usually erected in front of the shop in summer as a sunshade, which also attracted customers.

At a grand tree-planting activity in Beijing's Daxing County, a father and son plant trees together.

The photo exhibition "Founders of New China" attracts both adults and children.

A Currency Exchange Stall

In the 24 years between the end of the Qing Dynasty in 1911 and 1935, the money in circulation in China was silver and copper coins and banknotes; after 1935 the circulation of silver coins was banned, and replaced by paper currency, the denominations of which were equivalent to certain amounts of silver coins.

The exchange rate between copper coins and silver bills fluctuated. For daily expenses, copper coins were used more frequently, and ordinary people used to come to some stall to exchange money so the money exchange trade flourished. The Chinese characters written on the stall are "foreign dollar exchange." Here foreign dollars refer to the Mexican dollar minted abroad.

Advertisement for housing and car loans of the Agricultural Bank of China

Advertisement for sale of bonds in front of a bank

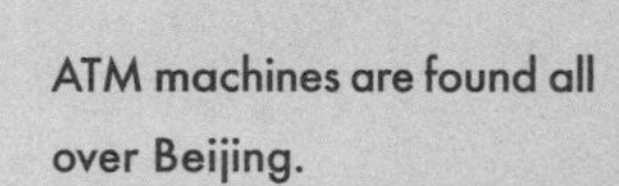

ATM machines are found all over Beijing.

Beijing's Financial Street

Collage Paintings

This is a kind of handicraft that combines painting with paper cutting and pasting. Pictures are painted in bright colors. Then they are cut out and pasted on a white sheet of paper, forming a landscape scenery or scene from a well-known fairy tale, novel or opera.

Dashanzi Art Gallery

Painting and calligraphy exhibition at the Yanhuang Museum of Art

The China Art Gallery and some of its exhibits

Candle Stall

Candles and candlesticks were indispensable at traditional sacrificial, wedding and funeral ceremonies. Different-colored candles were used for different occasions. Red candles were used for joyful occasions, such as weddings and birthdays, while white candles were used for sad occasions such as funeral ceremonies.

Teaching paper-cuts

There is a special compound in Pingxifu, suburb of Beijing where artists live and work away from the din and bustle of the city.

A Potter's Stall

Even though Beijing had a municipal water supply system, it was limited mainly to well-off families. The majority of common people used water from nearby wells, or bought it from water sellers. Almost all families needed a big vat to store water in. These earthenware vats were made in kilns outside Chaoyangmen and at Balizhuang in the western suburbs.

2004 CCTV Spring Festival Evening Get-Together Party

The 2005 New Year Concert, held at the Great Hall of the People

Bamboo and Wickerwork Stall

Common household items such as baskets, dust pans and sieves were made of bamboo or wickerwork, and were sold from stalls or by peddlers.

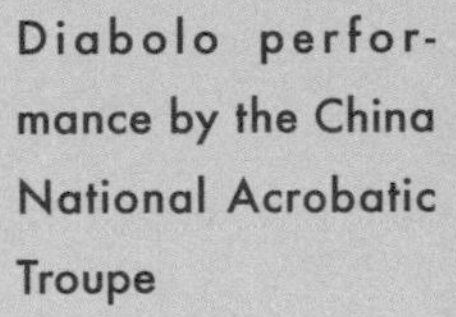

Diabolo performance by the China National Acrobatic Troupe

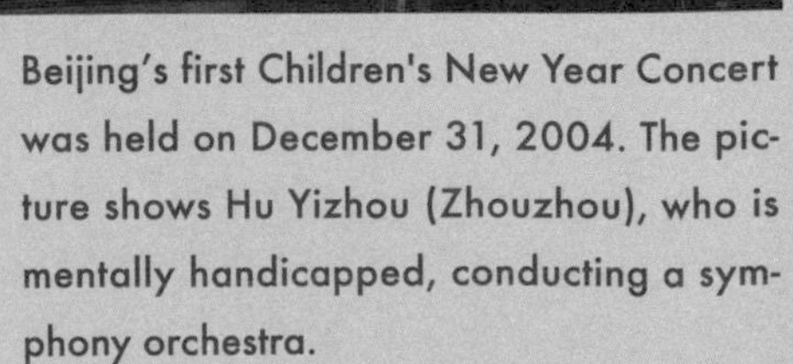

Beijing's first Children's New Year Concert was held on December 31, 2004. The picture shows Hu Yizhou (Zhouzhou), who is mentally handicapped, conducting a symphony orchestra.

Premiere of a new film

Selling Dusters

Beijing used to be a very dusty city, and so dusters were in great demand. In Beijing, they were usually made of rooster plumes bound to a rattan stick. There was also a kind of duster made of cloth strips used for dusting clothes and shoes. Towards the end of each year, the vendors would also sell dusters with extra-long handles for cleaning walls and ceilings.

A carnival parade at Beijing International Culture Tourism Festival

The 2004 "Wall of Hope" Concert held on the Great Wall

World-famous conductor Seiji Ozawa (left) at Beijing's Central Conservatory of Music

A vendor selling fans made of goose down

The opera *Aida* was staged at the Beijing Workers Stadium in September, 2003.

The opening ceremony of the French Culture Year was held in front of the Meridian Gate of the Forbidden City.

Beijing's Carpenters

As all Chinese traditional buildings contained a large amount of wood in their construction, and furniture was almost entirely made of wood, carpenters formed a large contingent of craftsmen. Many carpenters had special skills, and those who specialized in repairing furniture wandered the streets carrying their tools and touting for customers.

Despite the appearance of more and more modern buildings, the traditional ones have by no means lost their special charm and splendor.

The former residence of Peking Opera star Mei Lanfang

Making Carpenter's Glue

Carpenters used to make specially strong glue by boiling pigskin or fish bladders in water.

Traditional art in daily life

Spring in a courtyard

A typical *hutong*

Vegetable Sellers

Vegetable vendors usually bought their wares from vegetable merchants at Tianqiao, Ritan and Yuetan early in the morning, and peddled them in the alleyways, even taking them directly to the houses of regular customers. They always washed the vegetables in a stream or sprayed them with well water to make them look fresh before offering them for sale.

Wheat harvest in a suburb of Beijing

The Garden of Worldly Flowers [or "Grand World Flower Garden"] in the southern suburbs of Beijing provides everything from exotic flowers to agricultural tourism.

Makeshift Kitchen

It was common to set up a temporary stove at a construction site to prepare food and boil water for the workers.

Traditional kitchen ranges, rarely found in cities nowadays, have become popular decorations in fast-food restaurants.

The Rickshaw Boy

The life of the Beijing rickshaw boy is familiar to many people thanks to Lao She's eponymous novel. The rickshaw was called a "foreign vehicle," and the rickshaw boys "foreign vehicle pullers" because the rickshaw was introduced from Japan at the beginning of the 20th century. The better known rickshaw factories in Beijing were Xifuxing, Dongfuxing, Shuangheshun and Yuelai. Some rickshaw boys worked for private families, and drew a monthly salary; others roamed the streets looking for customers, with whom they bargained over the fair. Some boys owned their own rickshaws, while others rented vehicles from rickshaw pools where they paid a fixed amount of rent to the owner on a daily basis. The photo shows rickshaw boys waiting for customers in Goldfish Alley.

Rickshaw boy with his employer

Shijingshan Amusement Park

Bowl Repairer

Many of the people who repaired cracked or broken porcelain bowls and pottery jars came from the suburbs outside Yongdingmen. Like the itinerant barbers, they roamed the streets with the tools of their trade slung from a carrying pole. Their advent was announced by the tinkling of two small copper bowls hanging from the pole as they struck a copper plate. This artisan's tools included a bamboo bow, a drill with a diamond bit, a small iron bowl for pressing the bit, a small pair of pliers, and clips of various sizes. Tiny holes were first drilled along the edges of the broken pieces of the bowl to be repaired, using the bow to twirl the drill, and then copper clips were driven into the holes to secure the pieces, before putty was finally applied. There was a saying in those days: "Don't accept porcelain repair work if you don't have a diamond bit," meaning, you should know your limits.

Chaoyang Park

Chinese Ethnic Culture Park

The Bamboo Screen Repairer

Beijing residents used to hang a screen made of thin bamboo strips over the doorway in summer. With the door open, the screen would facilitate the circulation of air, while helping to keep flies and mosquitoes out. As summer drew near, bamboo screen store would send their apprentices out to find out who wanted old screens repaired or wished to buy new screens. Most of the artisans of this trade came from Zaoqiang County, Hebei Province.

The photo shows a bamboo screen store.

Beijing World Park

Aquatic sports club at Jinhaihu Lake

Blacksmiths at Work

Most blacksmith's workshops were in the southern part of the city, and some were outside the city wall.

Pet grooming has become a profession.

A pet competition

A dog fashion show

Feeding squirrels in a park

High-wire walking above the Great Wall

Many communities in Beijing are equipped with health-building facilities.

A Taiji (shadow boxing) performance of 10,000 people in Tian'anmen Square

The "Second Ethnic Young People's Wedding Ceremony" opened at the China Millennium Monu-

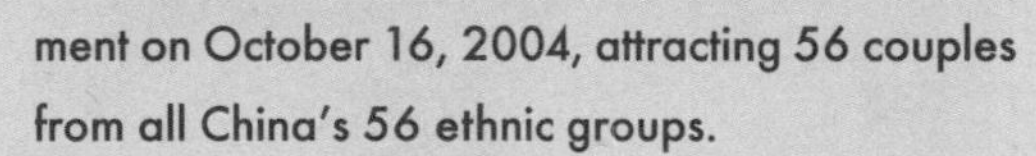

ment on October 16, 2004, attracting 56 couples from all China's 56 ethnic groups.

Blue roses imported from Holland were best sellers in the run up to Valentine's Day at Huaxiang Flower Market, Fengtai District.

With a bouquet of flowers

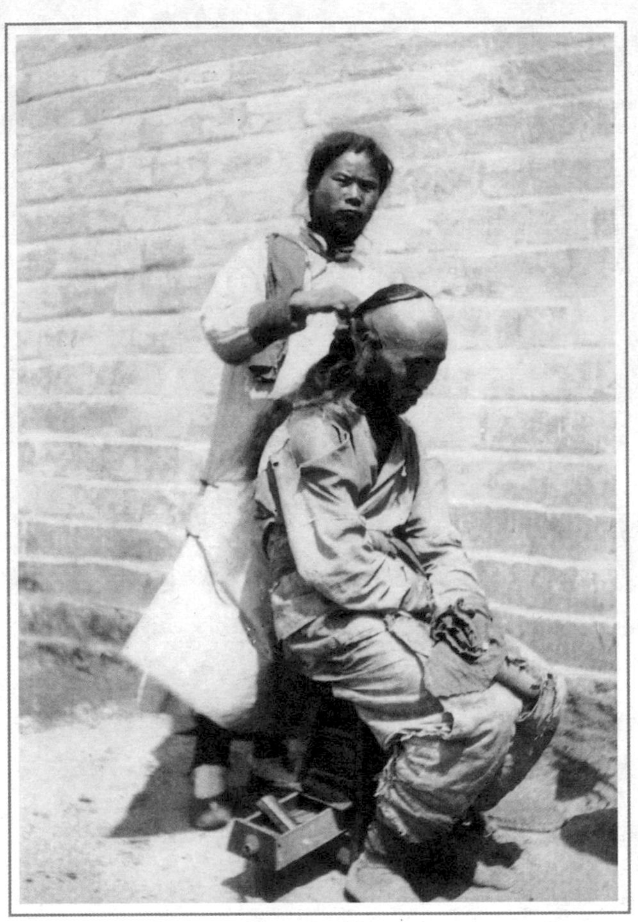

Barbers

The Manchu conquerors of China in the middle of the 17th century decreed that all Han men must shave off the hair in front of the head and let the rest of the hair grow long and be braided into a queue at the back. After the fall of Beijing, Dorgon, the Prince Regent, sent military barbers to force the Han people to adopt this style, upon pain of beheading. There was widespread resentment against this decree, and many men refused to be humiliated, preferring to lose their heads instead of their hair.

During the Qing Dynasty, barbers had to register with the local authorities before being allowed to ply their trade on the streets. These barbers were originally peasants from nearby Baodi, Sanhe and Wuqing counties. Their descendants carried on this trade for generations. The photo shows a barber, after shaving the front of his customer's head, braiding his queue.

Shaven-Head Style

After the fall of the Qing Dynasty in 1911, the queue hairstyle quickly went out of fashion. With the exception of men of the affluent classes and intellectuals, who preferred the Western hairstyle, most men had their heads completely shaven.

The itinerant barbers roamed the *hutong* and streets with a carrying pole, which had on one end a jug of water and a basin, and on the other a small cabinet with drawers for razors, combs, etc., and also served as a stool for customers. The itinerant barbers announced that they were in the neighborhood by twanging a tweezer-like fork, which produced a sound not unlike that of a bass violin.

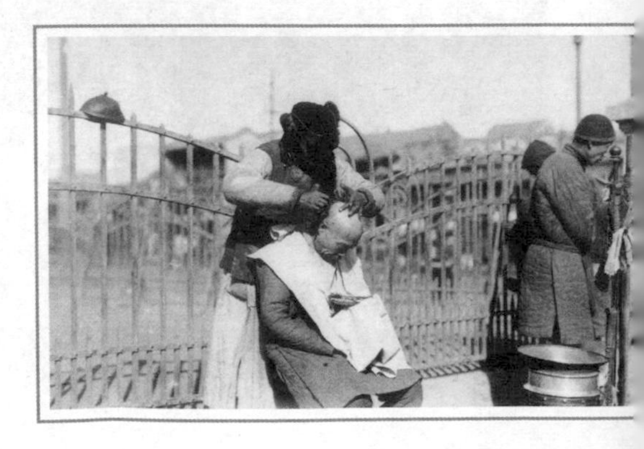

The official announcement of the 2004 Fashion, Hairstyle and Make-up Trends Show [part of the China International Fashion Week] was held in the Grand Ballroom of the Beijing Hotel.

Statues on Wangfujing Street

The Chinese entry in the Miss World Model contest

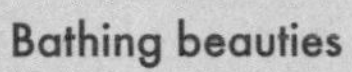
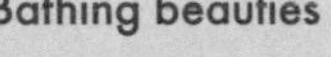

Bathing beauties

Fashion show

Miss World Model contestants visit the Forbidden City and *hutong*.

Paper *Yuanbao*

A *yuanbao* is a shoe-shaped gold or silver ingot used as money in ancient China. As a children's plaything, or as a propitious object to be displayed during the Chinese New Year, *yuanbao* made of gold or silver paper were sold. People used to hang strings of these as decorations. There were also paper cuts of propitious designs signifying happiness, wealth, health and longevity for sale during the New Year holidays. These paper products – either stuck onto iron sticks to insert into glutinous cakes, preserved fruits or other kinds of offerings, or stuck onto door lintels, shrines and windows, were mostly made and sold by stores on Huashi Street.

China's first Beauty & Hairdressing Contest held in Beijing

Health clubs have sprouted up all over Beijing.

Herman Cattaneo, a leading DJ from South America, who ranked sixth worldwide in 2004, performs at a discotheque in Beijing.

Hot spring resort in a suburb of Beijing

Thread Winding

A cotton-thread winder and his apprentice

Manipulating a 26-kg diabolo at the Longtanhu (Dragon Lake) Temple Fair

In Huangchenggen Cultural Relics Site Park

Fortune Teller

Fortune telling was popular all over old Beijing, but Tianqiao was the location of a particular concentration of fortune tellers. In 1915, there were eight fortune-telling studios and over 20 street stalls set up by fortune tellers. When Beijing was occupied by the Japanese invaders in 1937, the number of fortune tellers at Tianqiao increased to over 100. Chinese fortune-telling is based mainly on the *Yi Jing* (*Book of Changes*), certain medicinal knowledge, divination and astrology. Some fortune tellers were blind. The photo shows a fortune-teller's stall. In the center of the table is a container with bamboo strips used for divination.

The news of the successful launch of the Shenzhou V, China's first manned space mission, quickly spread over the city.

The new Beijing Planetarium opened in 2004.

The Bridal Sedan Chair

On the wedding day, the bridegroom's family sent a procession to bring the bride from her parents' home. Headed by men beating drums and gongs, the procession included people carrying red umbrellas, green-palm fans, dragon and phoenix flags, and the bridal sedan chair. For the remarriage of a widow or the marriage of a concubine, it was the custom to send a cart. In the Qing Dynasty, daughters of officials used sedan chairs covered with red woolen material, while commoner girls used embroidered cloth. From the 1930s, the sedan chair was covered with red satin with a phoenix-and-peony design. The photo shows peony-shaped streamers trailing out of the beak of a phoenix at each corner of the sedan chair and bearing propitious characters signifying "happy marriage."

Trousseau Procession

Delivering the trousseau was part of the complicated wedding etiquette of old Beijing. According to the established custom, the bride's trousseau and dowry had to be delivered to the groom's home on the afternoon before the wedding. On that day, four to eight men of the bride's family or family friends would escort a group of men carrying the trousseau. The objects were placed on stretchers, where they could be seen by the people in the street. Each stretcher was carried by two men. From a rich family the number of stretchers might be as high as 120 sets, forming a long procession.

Household utensils formed a large part of the trousseau and dowry, and as a rule they included a clock, potted plants, a make-up mirror, a long-necked porcelain vase with a feather duster inserted, a pair of candlesticks complete with red candles, a specially made lantern signifying longevity, a pair of tea containers, a pair of hat stands, and a pair of flower vases.

Rich families sometimes would present a new house to the couple, in which case a tile would be carried on a special stretcher. If a piece of land was given, a sun-dried mud brick with a piece of paper inscribed with the measurements of the land would be carried on its own stretcher – or a store sign board if a store was to be transferred to the new couple.

The photo shows a dressing table and a tea container on the first stretcher, and a clock and a vase on the second.

China's 1st Wedding Expo opened in Beijing on February 25, 2005.

Today, young people spend hundreds of times as much as their parents did on weddings.

Wedding photo

Nine "Beauty Leopard" cars in a wedding convoy on the first day of the first lunar month, 2005.

Pavilion-Like Structures with Inscriptions for the Dead

The obsequies for rich and official families involved intricate ceremonies, designed to show off their wealth and rank. The photo shows a procession carrying small pavilion-like structures with inscriptions for the dead carried by two men each at the head of a funeral procession. The structures were made with paper and light-weight material. The inscriptions were eulogies written by friends or relatives. Following these inscriptions were elegiac couplets and paper wreaths. The couplets were hung on bamboo poles carried in the procession, and the wreaths, presented by important personages, were hung on the four corners of the bier. Other wreaths were carried by people in the procession.

The Carrying Poles and the Coffin Cover

The carriers of a funeral bier could be 32, 48, or 64 in number. They shouldered wooden cylindrical poles painted with red lacquer. Half of the carriers walked in front of the bier and half behind. The outer frame of the coffin was covered with red embroidered brocade. On the four corners of the frame were four dragon heads, from which hung four woven tassels called *liusui*. Four yellow silk ribbons tied to the bier were pulled by four persons. This service was called *lahuang*, or "pulling the banner." On the top of the bier was a gilded wooden knob which symbolized fire.

If the deceased was to be brought from a narrow lane, smaller poles and a smaller cover were used, until the procession reached a wider road, when the regular-sized ones were substituted. During the changeover, the coffin was not supposed to be exposed.

The carriers of the bier would be changed in two or three shifts depending on the distance to the burial site. The leader of the carriers walked in front wearing a white robe and holding two wooden sticks which he beat against each other rhythmically so that the carriers could keep in step.

In the Qing Dynasty, the funeral of an emperor would call for 120 carriers. The men were positioned so that when viewed from above they formed a swastika-shaped pattern, with 32 men at each of the legs of the swastika. Everything should have an apricot-yellow color, the royal color. That is to say, the frame, the covering, the robes of the carriers, the carrying poles, and even the ropes were all of this color.

Funerals for members of the imperial family and high officials would entail 80, 64 or 48 carriers, but the apricot-yellow color was only used for the emperor and prices. For commoners, Manchu or Han, the number of carriers was limited to 80, and the color used was red. The coffin carrier service had a long history. Some successful coffin-carrying businesses were owned by people from Shanxi Province, and specialized in having Manchus for customers.

The Beijing carriers were specially trained to keep the coffin steady as the procession proceeded, and this technique was known and admired throughout the country. They were sometimes even invited to provide this service for people in other big cities.

Sina Invitational Golf Tournament

A golf course in Beijing's Changping District

The Artisans' Guild

The artisans' guilds in old Beijing were autocratic organizations, with the head of the guild wielding absolute power over the members. The largest guilds in Beijing were those of the masons and carpenters. The photo shows a meeting of a group of artisans before a teahouse.

The 1st Asian Color Forum

Caxa-Dassault Systemes Alliance Signing Ceremony

The 2nd International Finance Forum Annual Conference

Bean Curd Served with Sauce

On one end of the bean curd vendor's carrying pole was a tray of soybean sauce, fermented bean curd, sesame paste, chopped chives and hot-pepper sauce. On the other end was a bronze pot holding ready-made bean curd, underneath which was a small stove. When serving a customer, steaming hot bean curd was first placed in a bowl, and then the other ingredients were added in accordance with the customer's preference.

The 2004 China Trade Association Achievements Exhibition

China International Exhibition on Stadiums & Arenas and Sports & Leisure Infrastructure Supplies and Services

Fermented Bean Soup

This is a favorite Beijing specialty. It is made fermenting the residue of mung-bean noodles. The soup is served steaming hot, and has a grayish-green color and a sour taste. It used to be served at snack stalls and by peddlers in the street, and was often accompanied by salted pickles, crispy fried dough rings and sesame seed cakes. Fermented bean soup is a kind of appetizer, and helps the digestion.

Beijing International High-tech Expo

The 2nd China Agricultural Trade Fair

Fried Shrimps

The vendor had a small stove with a chimney on his cart. The shrimps were freshly fried for the customer, with ginger, onion and soy sauce added. This dish was commonly sold in the summer, when the vendors would go early in the morning to the moats around the city or to rivers in the suburbs to catch the shrimps.

People's lifestyles are changing along with high-tech development.

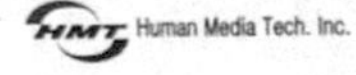
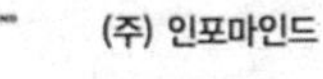

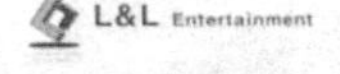

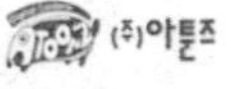

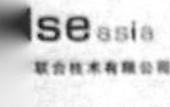

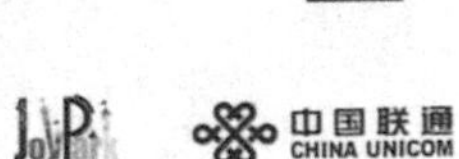

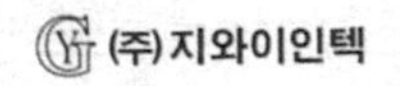

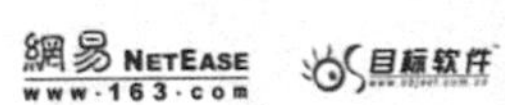

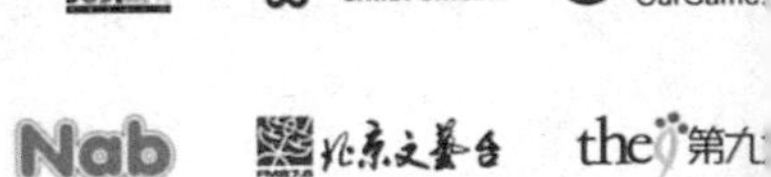

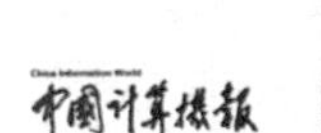

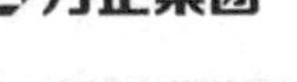

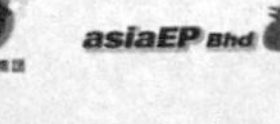

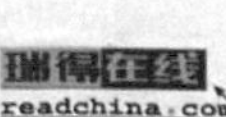

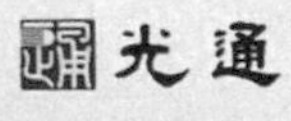

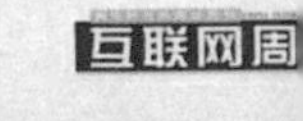
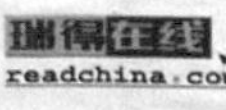

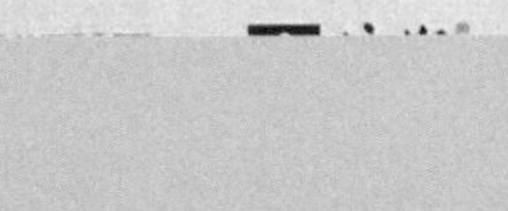

Peanuts and Persimmons

Peanuts are a common crop in Beijing's suburbs. The farmers would either come into the city to sell their peanuts themselves or sell them to vendors. The latter would sell them either roasted or raw. Persimmons were often sold by the same vendor, as the two crops mature in the same season.

Among the two kinds of persimmons in Beijing – the flat ones and the more rounded ones – those of Fangshan County in the western suburbs were known for their good quality. They were sold in early autumn, in September or October, and had to be soaked in boiling water to get rid of their puckery taste.

Shooting with a DV camera while riding a tandem

A scene as lovely as south of the Yangtze River

There are three seven-day "Golden Week" holidays every year, boosting tourism and mass consumption.

Experiencing farmers' life in a suburb of Beijing

Candied Fried Dough Twists

This cake is also known as "candied ear" as it looks like a human ear. Made of flour mixed with sugar, milk and oil, it is a favorite of the Islamic Hui people. It is deep-fried before being soaked in molasses for some time.

Together with fried glutinous cake and fried dough twist, it is one of the three typical Beijing snacks.

Old and young alike enjoy themselves in a quiet park.

Fishing in the suburbs of Beijing is becoming popular.

Ballroom dancing in the street is a common sight.

Glutinous Rice Cakes

Also known as "New Year cake," it is made of glutinous rice with sweetened bean paste and cooked dates, and is eaten together with finely cut red and green preserved fruits or haw jelly, as well as having sugar sprinkled on it. This is also a favorite of the Hui people, one of whom, by the name of Zhang, is shown in the photo, whose family engaged in the trade for generations. Another kind of snack called *Aiwowo* was often sold on the same stand of the glutinous-rice cake. It is a steamed glutinous-rice ball with sweetened bean past or sesame filling, mostly sold in spring and summer.

Tuanjiehu residential area

Changping, one of Beijing's satellite towns

Sweet Glutinous-Rice Dumplings

In Chinese, they are called *yuanxiao*, which means "the night of the fifteenth of the first lunar month." This is also the date of the Lantern Festival, and so the festival was also known as the "Sweet Dumpling Festival." The custom of eating sweet glutinous-rice dumplings on this particular day began in the fifth century BC. This spherical-shaped food for the yearly festival is popular also because it symbolizes togetherness and harmony.

The filling of the glutinous-rice dumplings in Beijing is sugar and haw jelly, sugar and osmanthus jelly, or sweetened bean paste, together with plums, sesame and walnuts. In southern China, the dumplings are called *tangtuan*, and can have a salty or even spicy flavor.

In Beijing, they are made by cutting the mixed fillings into small cubes, which are moistened and coated with glutinous-rice flour. The dumplings are about the size of walnuts.

In the old days, sweet glutinous-rice dumplings were boiled and served hot by vendors in the street.

New houses and villas in Hancunhe Village

A holiday resort in a suburb of Beijing

The Rice Gruel Vendor

The photo shows a vendor selling rice gruel at a temple fair. Such vendors also sold sesame cakes, fried dough twists and deep-fried doughnuts with the gruel in the morning in the street. All these together made a typical breakfast for the Beijing commoner.

The vendor could arrange his carrying pole to serve as a bench for his customers.

Seals add luster to traditional Chinese calligraphy and paintings.

Carving seals for customers on Liulichang Culture Street

A store selling the "four treasures of the study" (writing brush, ink, inkslab and paper) on Liulichang Culture Street

Bean Jelly

This dish is made of strips of white bean jelly, formed by pressing boiled bean paste through a funnel into cold water, and served with an assortment of ingredients: soybean sauce, vinegar, sesame paste, mustard, pounded garlic and chili oil. The dish is served cold, sometimes iced, and is still a favorite in the summer in Beijing.

Antique store

At an auction

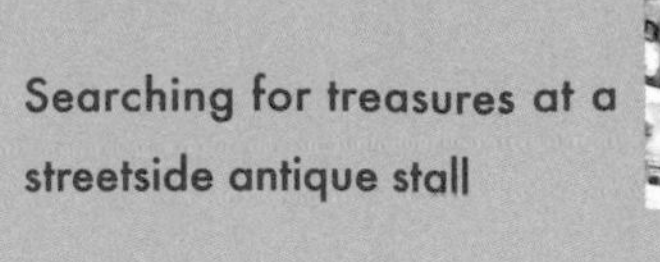

Searching for treasures at a streetside antique stall

Plum Juice

This was the most popular soft drink in the summer in Beijing. It was made with dried plums boiled in water, sugar and green plums. In the old days, this drink was served with cracked ice. The vendor would walk the streets clinking two small copper cups together in one hand to announce his approach. The vendor in the photo also sells cigarettes. Customers lit their cigarettes from the cone-shaped incense stick.

Behind the vendor is a watermelon stand, a common sight in Beijing during the summer.

Chatang is a traditional Beijing snack.

Sugar-Coated Haws Strung on a Stick

Called *tanghulu* in Chinese, these sweets, popular with children and adults alike, could also be made with crabapples, water chestnuts, tangerines or yams instead of haws. They were sold mostly in winter at temple fairs. Usually, the stick was less than a foot long, but during the Spring Festival there were also haw-*tanghulu* three times as long, each topped with a colorful flag.

Guijie: Food and Beverage Street springs to life at night.

Guijie offers a great diversity of dishes.

Beef and Mutton Cooked with Soybean Paste

Most of the cooks and vendors of beef and mutton dishes were Islamic Hui people. They also sold ox and mutton heads, and tripe. All these dishes were made with soybean sauce and various kinds of spices, and simmered over a low fire. A restaurant called Yueshengzhai outside Zhengyangmen was particularly famous for these dishes.

A counter selling imported kitchen utensils

Stylish show window

New Dong'an Mall

The Muskmelon Seller

Muskmelon, of which there are several kinds, is called "sweet and fragrant melon" in Chinese. It is a popular thirst-quencher in the summer.

The vendor would cut a chunk out of a melon for a prospective customer using a thin copper coin, to show whether it was ripe or not.

Sculptures decorate certain streets.

Open-Air Teahouse

Teahouses were important places for leisurely gatherings in old Beijing. The big traditional teahouses gradually disappeared after 1900, and smaller ones which also served snacks became popular. In the 1930s and 1940s, small and middle-sized teahouses sprang up in Tianqiao, some of which served tea only and were often patronized early in the morning by old men out for a walk carrying caged birds for exercise. In some of these teahouses, story tellers used to perform.

The photo shows a simple type of open-air teahouse which served mostly retired old men, and craftsmen and other people of the lower classes.

Lao She Teahouse

A young customer enjoying fragrant tea

Twins perform the Chinese tea ceremony of the Er Mei School at the annual early spring tea market.

Night life in Shichahai

An old railway carriage converted into a tavern on Sanlitun Bar Street

Bars, cafes and teahouses can be found everywhere in Beijing.

Peking Opera: *The Commander Who Wanted to Execute His Own Son*

This is a scene from a Peking opera performance in the early years of the 20th century. Beijing was where this kind of opera developed into a brilliant theatrical performing art, after three Anhui opera troupes came to perform for the emperor 200 years ago. Many generations of actors spent their whole life on the stage, perfecting the art little by little. Many became masters of different schools of performance, including Cheng Changgeng, Wang Xiaonong, Tan Xinpei, Yu Shuyan and Mei Lanfang. As Peking opera grew in popularity, more theaters were built. The oldest one was the Guangheyuan Theater. It was set up as a teahouse, with benches arranged around the stage. The audience sipped tea while watching the performances. The Jixiang Theater on Wangfujing Street was the first modern-style theater in Beijing, with rows of seats arranged facing the stage. The Kaiming Theater, built in 1912, was a Western-style theater. Later ones, like the Chang'an Theater, built in 1933, were more modernized, and all had a seating capacity of over 1,000.

Scene from *Where Three Roads Meet*, a Peking opera

Dou Erdun, a *jing* (robust figure) role in the Peking opera *Stealing the Imperial Horse*

Mei Lanfang–World Famous Peking Opera Actor

The photo shows Mr. Mei Lanfang in the role of Han Yuniang in the opera *Bitterness in Life and Death*, staged in 1935. Mei, who specialized in young female roles and sang in a falsetto voice, was the first Peking opera actor to gain international fame. He performed in the United States, the Soviet Union and Japan, and was offered a doctorate by an American university. He made great contributions to the performing arts, and established a school of Peking opera with followers not only on China's mainland but also in Hong Kong, Taiwan and among overseas Chinese.

Sun Shangxiang, a *dan* (female) role in the Peking opera *Prosperity Brought by the Dragon and the Phoenix*

Itinerant Opera Performers

Performers who were not attached to celebrated troupes used to perform in tea houses, at temple fairs, on impromptu stages or on street corners. The photo shows the leading role player of an itinerant troupe accompanied by a group of young apprentices.

Traditional peepshows with singing and commentary

Stilt Performers

Performances of folk tales and historical stories were sometimes given by troupes skilled at walking on stilts so that they could be seen above the heads of the crowd at temple fairs and suchlike gatherings. The photo shows a long-haired Buddhist monk, followed by an old fisherman and his wife, a woodcutter, a peasant, and a stupid scholar and his wife. The performances were accompanied by drums and gongs. Some performers could even turn somersaults on stilts.

Stilt-walking at a temple fair

Temple fair held in Grand View Garden Park

Lion Dance

The first mention of the Lion Dance known dates back to the Tang Dynasty (618-907), when the poet Bai Juyi mentioned it in one of his poems.

The Beijing Lion Dance belongs to the northern school (the southern school is represented by the Guangdong Lion Dance). In the northern style, two persons impersonate the lion, with one man manipulating the head, and the other the tail. A third performer tosses an embroidery ball, enticing the lion to move this way and that, to the accompaniment of drums and gongs. Lion Dance performances, usually by amateurs, were a feature of the annual temple fairs.

"The Longest Dragon in the North," 40 m long, made by China National Arts & Crafts Corp.

Ditan (Altar of the Earth) Temple Fair

Lion dance performance at a festival

Rhythmic Storytelling

This form of entertainment, known as *shulaibao*, used to be accompanied by the clapping of two pieces of bone. Later, bamboo clappers were used.

In the photo, the performer holds two large bamboo clappers in his left hand and five small ones in his right hand.

Toy Windmills

Toy windmills made of paper are still sold during the Spring Festival (Chinese New Year) at temple fairs. The colorful windmill turns in the breeze, causing two bamboo sticks to beat a small drum.

The annual Grand Assembly of Ancient Banners was held in Mentougou District on the 15th and 16th days of the first lunar month, 2005. The picture shows the banner team going through a village.

A *Qigong* Performance at Tianqiao—Swallowing a Sword

Qigong is a Chinese system of breathing exercises and is part of the Chinese martial arts, known as *kungfu*. Sword swallowing is related to *qigong*, which purports to allow an adherent to relax his esophagus sufficiently to allow him to swallow a sharp instrument such as a sword.

A girl enjoying herself at the "Building Ecological Civilization Exhibition," organized by Beijing Zoo

Trident Acrobatics

The trident is an ancient weapon, and manipulating a trident is an exercise in the repertoire of the Chinese martial arts. It involves rolling the weapon around the body continuously. The most famous exponent of this skill at Tianqiao was an old man named Tan Junchuan, who used to perform stripped to the waist even in the depth of winter.

Mickey and Minnie Mouse on the Great Wall

Learning to make *jiaozi* (Chinese dumplings)

Captivated by *hutong* life

The City Walls and City Gates of Old Beijing

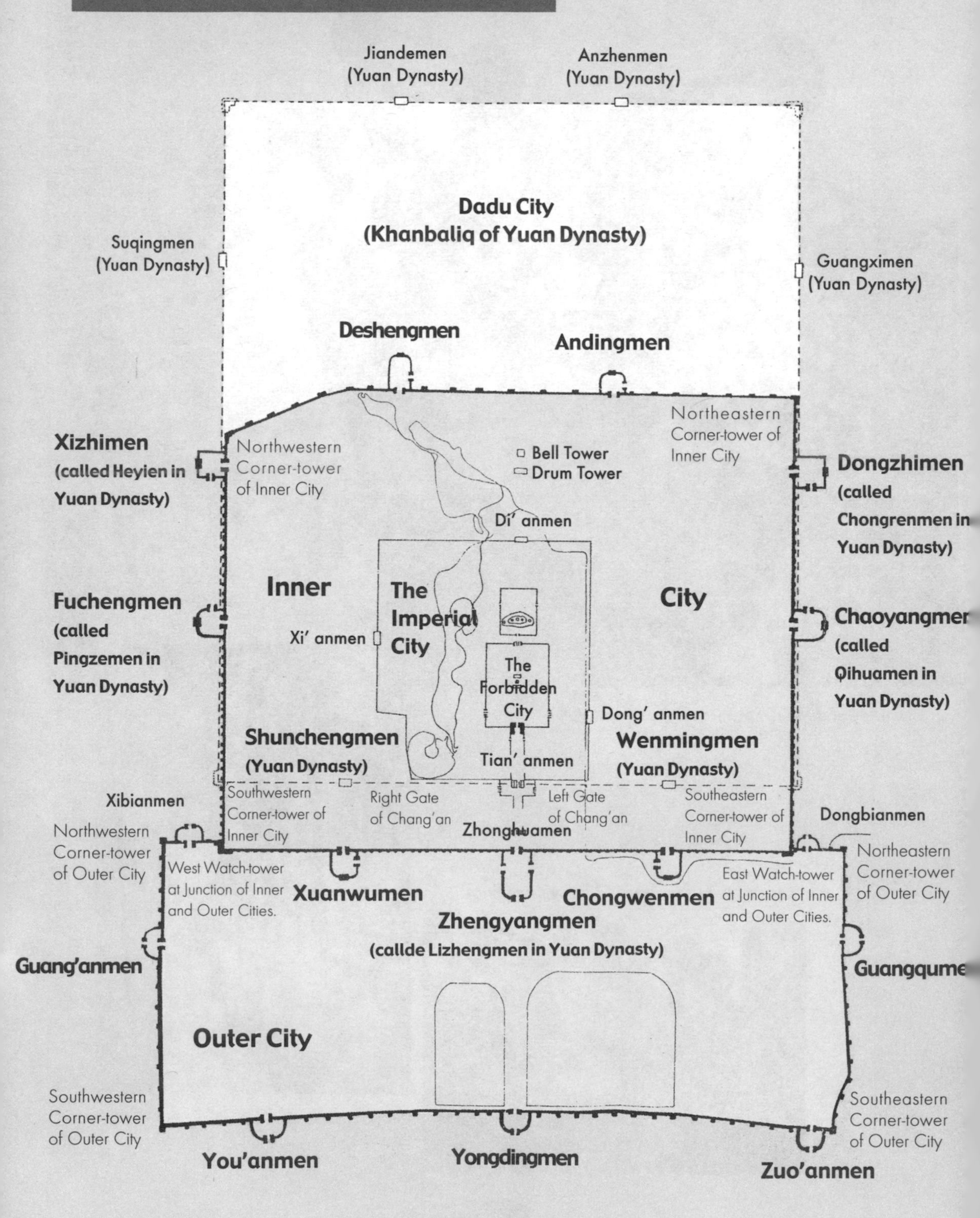

Embassies in Beijing

Albania, Embassy of Republic of

Add: 28 Guanghua Lu, Jianguomenwai, Chaoyang District

Tel: 6532 1120

Algeria, Embassy of Democratic People's Republic of

Add: 7 Sanlitun Lu, Chaoyang District

Tel: 6532 1231

Angola, Embassy of Republic of

Add: 1-13-1 Tayuan Diplomatic Office Building, Jianguomenwai

Tel: 6532 6968

Argentina, Embassy of Republic of

Add: 11 Dongwu Lu, Sanlitun, Chaoyang District

Tel: 6532 2090

Armenia, Embassy of Republic of

Add: 4-1-61, Tayuan Diplomatic Building, Jianguomenwai

Tel: 6532 5677

Australia, Embassy of

Add: 21 Dongzhimenwai Dajie, Chaoyang District

Tel: 6532 2331-7 Fax: 6532 4605

Austria, Embassy of Republic of

Add: 5 Xiushui Nanjie, Jianguomenwai, Chaoyang District

Tel: 6532 2061 - 3, 6532 1777

Azerbijan, Embassy of Republic of

Add: 2-10-2, Tayuan Diplomatic Office Building, Jianguomenwai

Tel: 6532 4614

Bahrain, Embassy of the State of

Add: 2-9-1, Tayuan Diplomatic Office Building, Jianguomenwai

Tel: 6532 5025/8, 6532 5017

Bangladesh, Embassy of People's Republic of

Add: 42 Guanghua Lu, Jianguomenwai

Tel: 6532 2521, 6532 3706

Belarus, Embassy of the Republic of

Add: 2-10-1, Tayuan Diplomatic Office Building, Jianguomenwai

Tel: 6532 6426

Belgium, Embassy of

Add: 6 Sanlitun Lu, Chaoyang District

Tel: 6532 1736 - 8, 6532 2782 Fax: 6532 3507

Benin, Embassy of the Republic of

Add: 38 Guanghua Lu, Jianguomenwai

Tel: 6532 2741, 6532 3122, 6532 2302 (Secretary)

Bolivia, Embassy of the Republic of

Add: 2-3-2, Tayuan Diplomatic Office Building, Jianguomenwai

Tel: 6532 4370, 6532 3074

Botswana, Embassy of the Republic of

Add: 1-8-1, 1-8-2, Tayuan Diplomatic Office Building,Jianguomenwai

Tel: 6532 5751 - 6

Brazil, Embassy of the Federative Republic of

Add: 27 Guanghua Lu, Jianguomenwai

Tel: 6532 2881, 6532 3883

Brunei Darussalam, Embassy of

Add: 1-91, Sanlitun Diplomatic Office Building

Tel: 6532 4094

Bulgaria, Embassy of the Republic of

Add: 4 Xiushui Beijie, Jianguomenwai

Tel: 6532 1946, 6532 1916, 6532 4925 (Commercial Section)

Burundi, Embassy of the Republic of

Add: 25 Guanghua Lu, Jianguomenwai

Tel: 6532 2328, 6532 1801

Cambodia, Royal Embassy of

Add: 9 Dongzhimenwai Dajie, Chaoyang District

Tel: 6532 1889, 6532 1958

Cameroon, Embassy of the Republic of

Add: 7 Dongwu Lu, Sanlitun, Chaoyang District

Tel: 6532 1828, 6532 2119 6532 2226 (Ambassador)

Canada, Embassy of

Add: 19 Dongzhimenwai Dajie, Chaoyang District

Tel: 6532 3536

Chad, Embassy of the Republic of

Add: 21 Guanghua Lu, Jianguomenwai

Tel: 6532 1295 / 6, 6532 4830

Chile, Embassy of the Republic of

Add: 1 Dongsi Jie, Sanlitun, Chaoyang District

Tel: 6532 1591, 6532 2074, 6532 1641 (Ambassador), 6532 1287

Columbia, Embassy of the Republic of

Add: 34 Guanghua Lu, Jianguomenwai

Tel: 6532 3377, 6532 1713, 6532 3166 (Consular Section)

Congo, Embassy of the Republic of

Add: 7 Dongsi Jie, Sanlitun, Chaoyang District

Tel: 6532 1658

Cote d'Ivoire, Embassy of the Republic of

Add: 9 Beixiaojie, Sanlitun

Tel: 6532 1223, 6532 3192

Croatia, Embassy of the Republic of

Add: 2-1-31, Diplomatic Office Building, Sanlitun

Tel: 6532 6241, 6532 6256

Cuba, Embassy of the Republic of

Add: 1 Xiushui Nanjie, Jianguomenwai

Tel: 6532 1714, 6532 2349, 6532 6656 (Commercial Section)

Cyprus, Embassy of the Republic of

Add: 2-13-2, Tayuan Diplomatic Office Building

Tel: 6532 5057

Czech Republic, Embassy of

Add: Ritan Lu, Jianguomenwai

Tel: 6532 1531, 6532 6902 Fax: 6532 4814

Danish Embassy, Royal

Add: 1 Dongwu Jie, Sanlitun, Chaoyang District

Tel: 6532 2431

Ecuador, Embassy of the Republic of

Add: 11-2-1, Tayuan Diplomatic Office Building, Jianguomenwai

Tel: 6532 3158, 6532 3849, 6532 2264 (Residence)

Egypt, Embassy of the Arab Republic of

Add: 2 Ritan Donglu, Jianguomenwai

Tel: 6532 1825, 6532 1880, 6532 1920 (Commercial Section)

Equatorial Guinea, Embassy of the Republic of

Add: 2 Dongsi Jie, Sanlitun, Chaoyang District

Tel: 6532 3679

Eritrea, Embassy of the Republic of

Add: 1-4-2, Tayuan Diplomatic Office Building

Tel: 6532 6534

Ethiopia, Embassy of the Federal Democratic Republic of

Add: 3 Xiushui Nanjie, Jianguomenwai

Tel: 6532 1782, 6532 1721

Finland, Embassy of the Republic of

Add: 1-10-1, Tayuan Diplomatic Office Building

Tel: 6532 1817, 6467 8084 (Commercial Section 1) Fax: 6532 1884

France, Embassy of the Republic of

Add: 3 Dongsanjie, Sanlitun, Chaoyang District

Tel: 6532 1274, 6501 4868 (Commercial Section)

Gabon, Embassy of the Republic of

Add: 36 Guanghua Lu, Jianguomenwai

Tel: 6532 2810, 6532 3824, 6532 2621 (Ambassador)

Germany, Embassy of the Federal Republic of

Add: 5 Dongzhimenwai Dajie, Sanlitun, Chaoyang District

Tel: 6532 2161-5 Fax: 6532 5336

Ghana, Embassy of the Republic of

Add: 8 Sanlitun Lu, Chaoyang District

Tel: 6532 1319, 6532 1544, 6532 2296 (Ambassador)

Greece (Hellenic), Embassy of the Republic of

Add: 19 Guanghua Lu, Jianguomenwai

Tel: 6532 1317, 6532 1391, 6532 1588

Guinea, Embassy of the Republic of

Add: 2 Xiliujie St., Sanlitun

Tel: 6532 3649

Guyana, Embassy of the Cooperative Republic of

Add: 1 Xiushui Dongjie, Jianguomenwai

Tel: 6532 1337, 6532 1601 (Ambassador)

Hungary, Embassy of the Republic of

Add: 10 Dongzhimenwai Dajie, Chaoyang District

Tel: 6532 1431 - 3, 6532 3845 (Commercial Section)

Iceland, Embassy of the Republic of

Add: Unit 1005 / 6, Landmark Building, 8 North Dongsanhuan Lu

Tel: 6502 7706

India, Embassy of the Republic of

Add: 1 Ritan Donglu, Jianguomenwai

Tel: 6532 1908, 6532 1856, 6532 1927 (Ambassador)

Indonesia, Embassy of the Republic of

Add: Diplomatic Office Building, Sanlitun

Tel: 6532 5489, 6532 5484 - 8

Iran, Embassy of the Islamic Republic of

Add: 13 Dongliu Jie, Sanlitun, Chaoyang District

Tel: 6532 2040, 6532 1881 (Ambassador), 6532 2149

Iraq, Embassy of the Republic of

Add: 25 Xiushui Beijie, Jianguomenwai

Tel: 6532 3385, 6532 1873

Ireland, Embassy of

Add: 3 Ritan Nanlu, Jianguomenwai

Tel: 6532 2691, 6532 2914, 6532 2888 (Commercial Section)

Israel, Embassy of

Add: Rm. 405, West Wing Office Building, C.W.T.C., 1 Jianguomenwai Dajie Tel: 6505 0328, 6505 2970 - 2

Italy, Embassy of the Republic of

Add: 2 Dong'erjie, Sanlitun, Chaoyang District

Tel: 6532 2131 - 5, 6532 1540 (Ambassador) Fax: 6532 4676

Ivory Coast, Embassy of the Republic of

Add: 9 Beixiaojie, Sanlitun, Chaoyang District

Tel: 6532 1482, 65323572

Japan, Embassy of

Add: 7 Ritan Lu, Jianguomenwai

Tel: 6532 2361, 6532 2121

Jordan, Embassy of the Hashemite Kingdom of

Add: 5 Dongliu Jie, Sanlitun, Chaoyang District

Tel: 6532 3906, 6532 3283

Kazakhstan, Embassy of the Republic of

Add: 9 Dongliu Jie, Sanlitun, Chaoyang District

Tel: 6532 6182 - 3, 6532 6541, 6532 6536 (Commercial Section)

Kenya, Embassy of the Republic of

Add: 4 Xiliu Jie, Sanlitun, Chaoyang District

Tel: 6532 3381, 6532 2473, 6532 3325 (Ambassador)

Korea, Embassy of the Democratic People's Republic of

Add: Ritan Beilu, Jianguomenwai

Tel: 6532 1186, 6532 1154 (Protocol)

Korea, Embassy of the Republic of

Add: 3-4 / F, China World Trade Center, 1 Jianguomenwai Dajie

Tel: 6505 2608 - 9, 6505 3171

Kuwait, Embassy of the State of

Add: 23 Guanghua Lu, Jianguomenwai

Tel: 6532 2216, 6532 2182

Kyrghyzstan, Embassy of the Republic

Add: 2-4-1, Tayuan Diplomatic Office Building

Tel: 6532 6458 / 9

Lao People's Democratic Republic, Embassy of

Add: 11 Dongsi Jie, Sanlitun, Chaoyang District

Tel: 6532 1224

Lebanon, Embassy of

Add: 51 Dongliu Jie, Sanlitun

Tel: 6532 2197, 6532 3281, 6532 1560

Lesotho, Embassy of the Kingdom of

Add: 1-7-1, Tayuan Diplomatic Office Building

Tel: 6532 6842

Liberia, Embassy of the Republic of

Add: 2-5-2, Tayuan Diplomatic Office Building

Tel: 6532 5617

Libyan Arab Jamahiriya, the People's Bureau of the Great Socialist People's

Add: 3 Dongliu Jie, Sanlitun, Chaoyang District

Tel: 6532 3666

Lithuania, Embassy of the Republic of

Add: 8-2-12, Tayuan Diplomatic Office Building, Jianguomenwai

Tel: 6532 4421

Luxembourg, Embassy of the Grand-Duchy of

Add: 21 Neiwubu Jie

Tel: 6513 5937

Madagascar, Embassy of the Republic of
Add: 3 Sanlitun Dongjie, Sanlitun
Tel: 6532 1353, 6532 1643

Malaysia, Embassy of
Add: 13 Dongzhimenwai Dajie
Tel: 6532 2531 - 3 Fax: 6532 5032

Mali, Embassy of the Republic of
Add: 8 Dongsijie, Sanlitun
Tel: 6532 1704, 6532 1687, 6532 1618

Malta, Embassy of the Republic of
Add: 2-1-22, Tayuan Diplomatic Office Building, Jianguomenwai
Tel: 6532 3114

Marshall Islands, Embassy of the Republic of the
Add: 2-14-1, Tayuan Diplomatic Office Building, Jianguomenwai
Tel: 6532 5819, 6532 5904

Mauritius, Embassy of the Republic of
Add: 2-6-2, Tayuan Diplomatic Office Building, Jianguomenwai
Tel: 6532 5695

Mauritania, Embassy of the Islamic Republic of
Add: 9 Dongsanjie, Sanlitun, Chaoyang District
Tel: 6532 1346, 6532 1703, 6532 1685

Mexican States, Embassy of the United
Add: 5 Dongwu Jie, Sanlitun
Tel: 6532 2574, 6532 2070, 6532 2657 (Ambassador and Protocol)

Moldova, Embassy of the Republic of
Add: 2-4-2, Tayuan Diplomatic Office Building, Jianguomenwai
Tel: 6532 5494

Mongolia, Embassy of
Add: 2 Xiushui Beijie, Jianguomenwai
Tel: 6532 1203, 6532 1810 (Protocol), 6532 1952 (Commercial Section)

Morocco, Embassy of the Kingdom of
Add: 16 Sanlitun Dajie, Chaoyang District
Tel: 6532 1796, 6532 1483 / 9, 6532 1453

Mozambique, Embassy of the Republic of
Add: 1-7-1, Tayuan Diplomatic Office Building
Tel: 6532 3664, 6532 3578

Namibia, Embassy of the Republic of
Add: 1-13-2, Tayuan Diplomatic Office Building, Jianguomenwai
Tel: 6532 4810 Fax: 6532 4549

Nepalese Embassy, Royal
Add: 1 Xiliu Jie, Sanlitun
Tel: 6532 1795, 6532 3251, 6532 2739 (Ambassador) Fax: 6532 3251

Netherlands Embassy, Royal
Add: 4 Liangmahe Nanlu
Tel: 6532 1131 - 4 Fax: 6532 4689

New Zealand, Embassy of
Add: 1 Dong'er Jie, Ritan Lu, Jianguomenwai
Tel: 6532 2731 - 3 Fax: 6532 4317

Nigeria, Embassy of the Federal Republic of
Add: 2 Dongwu Jie, Sanlitun, Chaoyang District
Tel: 6532 3631 - 3, 6532 1650 Fax: 6532 1650

Norwegian Embassy, Royal
Add: 1 Dongyi Jie, Sanlitun, Chaoyang District
Tel: 6532 2261 / 2, 6532 1329, 6532 1426 (Ambassador) Fax: 6532 2392

Oman, Embassy of the Sultanate of
Add: 6 Liangmahe Nanlu
Tel: 6532 3692 Fax: 6532 5030

Pakistan, Embassy of the Islamic Republic of
Add: 1 Dongzhimenwai Dajie
Tel: 6532 2504, 6532 2695, 6532 6660, 6532 2581

Palestine, Embassy of the State of
Add: 2 Dongsan Jie, Sanlitun
Tel: 6532 1361, 6532 3241 Fax: 6532 3241

Papua New Guinea, Embassy of
Add: 2-11-2, Tayuan Diplomatic Office Building
Tel: 6532 4312, 6532 4709 Fax: 6532 5483

Peru, Embassy of the Republic of
Add: 2-82, Sanlitun Diplomatic Office Building
Tel: 6532 4658, 6532 3719, 6532 2976 (Commercial Section)

Philippines, Embassy of the Republic of the
Add: 23 Xiushui Beilu, Jianguomenwai
Tel: 6532 2794, 6532 1872, 6532 2518 Fax: 6532 3761

Poland, Embassy of the Republic of

Add: 1 Ritan Lu, Jianguomenwai

Tel: 6532 1235, 6532 1246 (Military Section) Fax: 6532 1745

Portugal, Embassy of the Republic of

Add: 2-15-1/2, Tayuan Diplomatic Office Building

Tel: 6532 3497, 6532 3242 Fax: 6532 4637

Qatar, Embassy of the State of

Add: 1-9-2, Tayuan Diplomatic Office Building

Tel: 6532 2231 - 5 Fax: 6532 5274

Romania, Embassy of

Add: Ritan Lu, Dong'er Jie

Tel: 6532 3442, 6532 3255 Fax: 6532 5728

Russian Federation, Embassy of the

Add: 4 Beizhong Jie, Dongzhimen, Sanlitun

Tel: 6532 2051, 6532 1381, 6532 1267 (Consular Section)

Rwanda, Embassy of the Republic of

Add: 30 Xiushui Beilu, Jianguomenwai

Tel: 6532 2193, 6532 1762 Fax: 6532 2006

Saudi Arabia, Royal Embassy of

Add: 1 Beixiao Jie, Sanlitun

Tel: 6532 4825, 6532 5325 Fax: 6532 5324

Senegal, Embassy of the Republic of

Add: 1 Ritan Dongyi Jie, Jianguomenwai

Tel: 6532 2593, 6532 2646

Sierra Leone, Embassy of the Republic of

Add: 7 Dongzhimenwai Dajie, Sanlitun

Tel: 6532 1222, 6532 2174 Fax: 6532 3752

Singapore, Embassy of the Republic of

Add: 1 Xiushui Beilu, Jianguomenwai

Tel: 6532 3926, 6532 3143 Fax: 6532 2215

Slovak Republic, Embassy of the

Add: Ritan Lu, Jianguomenwai

Tel: 6532 1531 Fax: 6532 4814

Slovenia, Embassy of the Republic of

Add: 3-53, Jianguomenwai

Tel: 6532 6356 Fax: 6532 6358

Somali Republic, Embassy of the

Add: 2 Sanlitun Lu, Sanlitun

Tel: 6532 1752

Spain, Embassy of

Add: 9 Sanlitun Lu, Sanlitun

Tel: 6532 1986, 6532 3728, 6532 3742 (Ambassador's Secretary)

Sri Lanka, Embassy of the Democratic Socialist Republic of

Add: 3 Jianhua Lu, Jianguomenwai

Tel: 6532 1861 / 2 Fax: 6532 5426

South Africa, Embassy of the

Add: C801 Lufthansa Center, 50 Liangmaqiao Lu

Tel: 6465 1941

Sudan, Embassy of the Republic of

Add: 1 Dong'er Jie, Sanlitun

Tel: 6532 3715, 6532 2205 Fax: 6532 1280

Sweden, Embassy of

Add: 3 Dongzhimenwai Dajie

Tel: 6532 3331 Fax: 6532 5008

Switzerland, Embassy of

Add: 3 Dongwu Jie, Sanlitun

Tel: 6532 2736 - 8 Fax: 6532 4353

Syrian Arab Republic, Embassy of the

Add: 6 Dongsi Jie, Sanlitun

Tel: 6532 1372, 6532 1347, 6532 1563 (Ambassador)

Tanzania, Embassy of the United Republic of

Add: 8 Liangmahe Nanlu, Sanlitun

Tel: 6532 1491, 6532 1719 Fax: 6532 4351

Thai Embassy, Royal

Add: 40 Guanghua Lu, Jianguomenwai

Tel: 6532 1903, 6532 3955, 6532 5058 (Commercial Section)

Togo, Embassy of the Republic of

Add: 11 Dongzhimenwai Dajie

Tel: 6532 2202, 6532 2444 Fax: 6532 2055

Tunisian Republic, Embassy of the

Add: 1 Sanlitun Donglu

Tel: 6532 2435 / 6 Fax: 6532 5818

Turkey, Embassy of the Republic of

Add: 9 Dongwu Jie, Sanlitun

Tel: 6532 2347, 6532 2184, 6532 3846, 6532 2650   Fax: 6532 5480

Turkmenistan, Embassy of

Add: 1-15-2, Tayuan Diplomatic Office Building

Tel: 6532 6975   Fax: 6532 6976

Uganda, Embassy of the Republic of

Add: 5 Sanlitun Donglu, Sanlitun

Tel: 6532 1708   Fax: 6532 2242

Ukraine, Embassy of

Add: 11 Dongliu Jie, Sanlitun

Tel: 6532 6359   Fax: 6532 6765

United Arab Emirates, Embassy of the

Add: 1-9-1, Tayuan Diplomatic Office Building

Tel: 6532 2112, 6532 5083 - 5   Fax: 6532 5089

United Kingdom of Great Britain and Northern Ireland, Embassy of the

Add: 11 Guanghua Lu, Jianguomenwai

Tel: 6532 1961 - 4, 6532 1930, 6532 1937 - 9, 6501 1903

United States of America, Embassy of the

Add: 3 Xiushui Beilu, Jianguomenwai

Tel: 6532 3831   Fax: 6532 3297

Uruguay, Embassy of the Oriental Republic of

Add: 2-7-2, Tayuan Diplomatic Office Building

Tel: 6532 4445, 6532 4413   Fax: 6532 4357

Uzbekistan, Embassy of the Republic of

Add: 7 Beixiao Jie, Sanlitun

Tel: 6532 6305   Fax: 6532 6304

Venezuela, Embassy of the Republic of

Add: 14 Sanlitun Lu, Sanlitun

Tel: 6532 1295, 6532 2694   Fax: 6532 3817

Vietnam, Embassy of the Socialist Republic of

Add: 32 Guanghua Lu, Jianguomenwai

Tel: 6532 1155, 6532 5415   Fax: 6532 5720

Yemen, Embassy of the Republic of

Add: 5 Dongsan Jie, Sanlitun

Tel: 6532 1558, 6532 1793 (Ambassador)   Fax: 6532 4305

Yugoslavia, Embassy of the Federal Republic of

Add: Dongliu Jie, Sanlitun

Tel: 6532 3516, 6532 3016, 6532 1693, 6532 1593, 6532 1562

Zaire, Embassy of the Republic of

Add: 6 Dongwu Jie, Sanlitun

Tel: 6532 1995, 6532 2713

Zambia, Embassy of the Republic of

Add: 5 Dongsi Jie, Sanlitun

Tel: 6532 1554, 6532 1778, 6532 2058 Fax: 6532 1891

Zimbabwe, Embassy of the Republic of

Add: 7 Dongsan Jie, Sanlitun

Tel: 6532 3665, 6532 3397, 6532 3795, 6532 3964

Five-Star Hotels in Beijing

Beijing Asia Jinjiang Hotel

Add: 8 Xinzhong Xijie, Gongti Beilu, Chaoyang District

Tel: 86-10-65007788

Beijing China World Hotel

Add: 1 Jianguomenwai Dajie, Chaoyang District

Tel: 86-10-65052266

Beijing Chang An Grand Hotel

Add: 27 Huaweili, Chaoyang District

Tel: 86-10-67731234

Beijing Hotel

Add: 33 Dong Chang'an Jie

Tel: 86-10-65137766

Celebrity International Grand Hotel

Add: 99 Anli Lu, Chaoyang District

Tel: 86-10-64981166

Century Golden Resources Hotel

Add: 69 Banjing Lu, Haidian District

Tel: 86-10-88598888

Crown Plaza Hotel North Beijing

Add: Huilongguan, Changping District

Tel: 86-10-80799988

Fragrant Hill Golden Resources Commerce Hotel Beijing

Add: 59 Bei Zhenghuangqi, Haidian District

Tel: 86-10-62868888

Grand Hotel Beijing

Add: 35 Dong Chang'an Jie

Tel: 86-10-65137788

Grand Hyatt Hotel Beijing

Add: 1 Dong Chang'an Jie

Tel: 86-10-85181234

Great Wall Sheraton Hotel Beijing

Add: 10 Dongsanhuan Beilu, Chaoyang District

Tel: 86-10-65905566

Hilton Hotel Beijing

Add: 1 Dongfang Lu, Dongsanhuan Beilu

Tel: 86-10-64662288

Holiday Inn Crown Plaza Beijing

Add: 48 Wangfujing Dajie

Tel: 86-10-65133388

International Hotel Beijing

Add: 9 Jianguomennei Dajie

Tel: 86-10-65126688

Jade Palace Hotel Beijing

Add: 76, Zhichun Lu, Haidian District

Tel: 86-10-62628888

Jing Guang New World Hotel Beijing

Add: Hujialou, Chaoyang District

Tel: 86-10-65978888

Kempinski Hotel Beijing

Add: 50 Liangmaqiao Lu, Chaoyang District

Tel: 86-10-64653388

Kerry Center Hotel Beijing

Add: 1 Guanghua Lu, Chaoyang District

Tel: 86-10-65618833

King Wing Hotel Beijing- Beijing King Wing Hot Spring Hotel

Add: 17 Dongsanhuan Nanlu

Tel: 86-10-67668866/67656008

Kunlun Hotel Beijing

Add: 2 Xinyuan Nanlu, Chaoyang District

Tel: 86-10-65903388

Millennium Hotel Beijing

Add: 338 Guang'anmen Dajie, Xuanwu District

Tel: 86-10-63578888

New Century Hotel Beijing

Add: 6 Shouti Nanlu

Tel: 86-10-68492001

New Otani Hotel Beijing

Add: Jianguomenwai Dajie

Tel: 86-10-65125555

Peninsula Palace Hotel Beijing--Former Palace Hotel

Add: 8 Jinyu Hutong, Wangfujing

Tel: 86-10-85162888

Presidential Hotel Beijing

Add: 9 Fuchengmenwai Dajie, Xicheng District

Tel: 86-10-68005588

Prime Hotel Beijing

Add: 2 Wangfujing Dajie

Tel: 86-10-65136666

Tianlun Dynasty Hotel Beijing

Add: 50 Wangfujing Dajie

Tel: 86-10-65138888

Wangfujing Grand Hotel

Add: 57 Wangfujing Dajie

Tel: 86-01-65221188

Zhaolong Hotel Beijing--Great Dragon Hotel Beijing

Add: Gongti Beilu, Chaoyang District

Tel: 86-01-65972299

Four-Star Hotels in Beijing

Beijing Avic Hotel

Add: 2 Donghuan Nanlu, Chaoyang District

Phone: 86-10-65661188

Beijing Capital Hotel

Add: 3 Qianmen Dongdajie

Tel: 86-10-65129988

Beijing CCECC Plaza Hotel

Add: 6 Beifengwo, Haidian District

Tel: 86-10-63246666

Beijing Chengyuan Hotel

Add: 19, Jianhua Nanlu, Jianguomenwai Dajie, Chaoyang District

Tel: 86-10-65677799

Beijing Continental Grand Hotel--Wuzhou Crown Plaza Hotel

Add: 8 Beichen Donglu

Tel: 86-10-84985588

Beijing CTS Tower--China Travel Service Tower

Add: 2 Beisanhuan Lu

Tel: 86-10-64622288

Beijing Debao Hotel

Add: 22 Debaoxinyuan, Xicheng District

Tel: 86-10-68318866

Beijing Dongjiaominxiang Hotel

Add: 23A Dongjiaomin Xiang, Dongcheng District

Tel: 86-10-65243311

Beijing Friendship Hotel

Add: 3 Baishiqiao Lu, Haidian District

Tel: 86-10-68498888

Beijing Gloria Plaza

Add: 2 Jianguomen Nandajie

Tel: 86-10-65158855

Beijing Grand View Hotel

Add: 88 Nancaiyuan Jie, Xuanwu District

Tel: 86-10-63538899

Beijing Guangxi Plaza Hotel

Add: 26 Huaweili Panjiayuan, Chaoyang District

Tel: 86-10-67796688

Beijing Jianguo Garden Hotel

Add: 19 Jianguomennei Dajie

Tel: 86-10-65286666

Beijing Jinglin Hotel

Add: 1. Nanping Dongli, Capital Airport

Tel: 86-10-64572626

Beijing Jinglun Hotel
Add: 3 Jianguomenwai Dajie
Tel: 86-10-65002266

Beijing Jinjian Hotel
Add: 2 Chaci, Dongzhimenwai Dajie
Tel: 86-10-64652255

Beijing Landmark Tower Hotel--Beijing Landmark Hotel
Add: 8 Dongsanhuan Beilu, Chaoyang District
Tel: 86-10-65906688

Beijing North Garden Hotel
Add: 218-1 Wangfujing Dajie
Tel: 86-10-65238888

Beijing Oriental Culture Hotel
Add: 101 Jiaodaokou Dongdajie, Dongcheng District
Tel: 86-10-84031188

Beijing Paragon Hotel—Howard Johnson Paragon hotel
Add: 18 Jianguomennei Dajie, Dongcheng District
Tel: 86-10-65266688

Beijing Plaza Hotel—Chuanbo Zhonggong Hotel
Add: 100 Dongsanhuan Nanlu, Chaoyang District
Tel: 86-10-67353366

Beijing Poly Plaza Hotel
Add: 14 Dongzhimen Nandajie, Dongcheng District
Tel: 86-10-65001188

Beijing Tianhong Plaza Hotel
Add: 25 Zhichun Lu, Haidian District
Tel: 86-10-82356699

Beijing Tibet Hotel
Add: 118 Beisihuan Donglu
Phone: 86-10-64981133

China Garment Hotel Beijing--Beijing Zhongfu Hotel
Add: 26 Dongzhimenwai Dajie
Tel: 86-10-64153388

China People's Palace Hotel Beijing
Add: 1 Zhenwumiao Lu, Xicheng District
Tel: 86-10-68576699

Guangzhou Hotel Beijing
Add: 3A Xidan Heng'ertiao
Tel: 86-10-66078866

Henan Plaza Hotel Beijing
Add: 28 Huaweili Panjiayuan, Chaoyang District
Tel: 86-10-67751188

Holiday Inn Chang An West Hotel Beijing
Add: 66 Yongding Lu
Tel: 86-10-68132299

Holiday Inn Lido Beijing
Add: Jichang Lu, Jiangtai Lu
Tel: 86-10-64376688

Jianguo Hotel Beijing
Add: 5 Jianguomenwai Dajie
Tel: 86-10-65002233

Jianshe Hotel Beijing
Add: A5 Guanglian Lu, Fengtai District
Tel: 86-10-63986611

Novotel Peace Hotel Beijing
Add: 3 Jinyu Hutong, Wangfujing
Tel: 86-10-65128833

Oriental Garden Hotel Beijing
Add: Dongzhimen Nandajie, Dongcheng District
Tel: 86-10-64168866

Radisson Hotel Beijing
Add: 6A Beisanhuan Donglu
Tel: 86-10-64663388

Rosedale Hotel Beijing--Former Harbor Plaza Beijing
Add: 8 Jiangtai Xilu, Chaoyang District
Tel: 86-10-64362288

Scitech Hotel (CVIK Hotel) Beijing

Add: 22 Jianguomenwai Dajie

Tel: 86-10-65123388

Shenzhen Hotel Beijing

Add: 1 Guang'anmenwai Dajie

Tel: 86-10-63271188

Sino-Swiss Hotel

Add: Xiaotianzhu Village, Shunyi District, Capital Airport

Tel: 86-10-64565588

Swissotel Beijing

Add: 2 Chaoyangmen Beilu

Tel: 86-10-65532288

Traders Hotel Beijing

Add: 1 Jianguomenwai Dajie

Tel: 86-10-65052277

Tsinghua Unisplendour International Center

Add: East Gate of Beijing Tsinghua University

Tel: 86-10-62791888

Wangfujing Grand Hotel

Add: 57 Wangfujing Dajie

Tel: 86-01-65221188

Xindadu Hotel

Add: 21 Chegongzhuang Dajie

Tel: 86-10-68319988

Xinqiao Hotel -- Novotel Xinqiao Hotel Beijing

Add: 2 Dongjiaomin Xiang

Tel: 86-10-65133366

Xiyuan Hotel

Add: 1 Sanlihe Lu, Xiyuan

Tel: 86-10-68313388

Yanshan Hotel

Add: 138A Zhongguancun Dajie

Tel: 86-10-62563388

Yongxing Garden Hotel Beijing

Add: 101 Fucheng Lu, Haidian District

Tel: 86-10-88111188

Yuyang Hotel Beijing

Add: 18 Xinyuanxili Zhongjie

Tel: 86-10-64669988

Zhejiang Plaza Beijing--Beijing Zhejiang Building

Add: 26 3rd District Anzhenxili

Tel: 86-10-64453388

Zhongyu Century Grand Hotel Beijing

Add: 31 Lianhuachi Donglu

Tel: 86-10-63989999

图书在版编目（CIP）数据

北京城与北京人／肖晓明策划，兰佩瑾编．－北京：外文出版社，2005（2007年重印）
（全景中国）
ISBN 978-7-119-04038-7
I.北…　II.①肖…②兰…　III.北京市－概况－英文IV.K921
中国版本图书馆CIP数据核字（2005）第039901号

全景中国——北京《北京城与北京人》

策　　划： 肖晓明
执行编辑： 兰佩瑾
前言撰稿： 徐城北
图片文字： 叶燕生　齐　放　祁汲然
图片提供： 北京市文物研究所　Photocome
张肇基　李少白　袁学军　王建华　王　志　杜殿文　高明义　何慷民
牛永利　许廷长　余　海　徐正荣　邓士平　刘利华　兰佩瑾

中文审定： 廖　频
责任编辑： 兰佩瑾
封面设计： 蔡　荣
内文设计： 元　青等
印刷监制： 韩少乙

出版发行：
外文出版社出版（中国北京百万庄大街24号）
邮政编码：100037　http://www.flp.com.cn
印　　制：
北京京都六环印刷厂
开本：980mm × 710mm 1/16(平装) 印张：15.875
2009年12月第1版第3次印刷
（英）
ISBN 978-7-119-04308-7
09800
85-E-577P